CASSELL STUDIES IN PASTORAL CARE AND PERSONAL
AND SOCIAL EDUCATION

MANAGING PASTORAL CARE

Edited by
Mike Calvert and Jenny Henderson

CASSELL

Cassell
Wellington House
125 Strand
London WC2R 0BB

PO Box 605
Herndon
VA 21605

First published 1998

British Library Cataloguing-in-Publication Data
A catalogue record for this book is available from the British Library.

ISBN 0-304-70067-3 (hardback)
 0-304-70068-1 (paperback)

Typeset by Fakenham Photosetting Ltd
Printed and bound in Great Britain by
Biddles Ltd, Guildford and King's Lynn

CASSELL STUDIES IN PASTORAL CARE AND PERSONAL
AND SOCIAL EDUCATION

MANAGING PASTORAL CARE

Other books in this series:

R. Best (editor): *Education, Spirituality and the Whole Child*

R. Best, P. Lang, C. Lodge and C. Watkins (editors): *Pastoral Care and Personal-Social Education: Entitlement and Provision*

G. Haydon: *Teaching about Values: A New Approach*

P. Lang, R. Best and A. Lichtenberg (editors): *Caring for Children: International Perspectives on Pastoral Care and PSE*

O. Leaman: *Death and Loss: Compassionate Approaches in the Classroom*

J. McGuiness: *Counselling in Schools: New Perspectives*

J. McGuiness: *Teachers, Pupils and Behaviour: A Managerial Approach*

L. O'Connor, D. O'Connor and Rachel Best (editors): *Drugs: Partnerships for Policy, Prevention and Education*

S. Power: *The Pastoral and the Academic: Conflict and Contradiction in the Curriculum*

J. Ungoed-Thomas: *Vision of a School: The Good School in the Good Society*

P. Whitaker: *Managing to Learn: Aspects of Reflective and Experiential Learning in Schools*

Contents

Series editors' foreword

In *Essential School Leadership* (Holmes, 1993), Gary Holmes argues that in any list of essentials for effective management in education, vision and purpose must be at the top. This is also the view taken in the Introduction to this book and is one which we wish to endorse. Without vision, one's purpose is likely to be restricted to the maintenance of the status quo or, at best, to piecemeal tinkering which may refine and improve performance but leave the parameters within which the organization functions fundamentally unexamined. Without purpose, vision remains a dream, unfocused and without clear targets or strategies for achieving them.

One may argue that vision and purpose express the eternal opposition between creativity, novelty and transcendence on the one hand and rationalism, realism and objectivism on the other. As in all things, we suppose good management to require both, balanced to achieve the optimum mix of conservatism and radicalism. It is a balance well struck in this book.

As the editors point out in their Introduction, the literature of pastoral care and PSE is not without some useful publications which deal directly with issues of management. Indeed, the early books in this field – Marland's (1974) *Pastoral Care* and Blackburn's (1975) *The Tutor* – might be seen to be precisely about this very thing. But they were conceived and developed from positions somewhat outside the academic community then identified with educational management and administration. Later books, including Blackburn's (1986) *Head of House, Head of Year* and Bell and Maher's (1986) *Leading a Pastoral Team* made significant advances in considering the management of that part of the school explicitly identified as 'pastoral'. Best *et al.*'s (1983) *Education and Care* and Sally Power's (1996) *The Pastoral and the Academic* brought an important sociological perspective to bear on the rhetoric and the reality of pastoral management. Several of the contributors to the standard text on *Pastoral Care and Personal-Social Education* (Best *et al.*, 1995; published in this series) address management issues, including the desirability of more organic pastoral bureaucracies (Lodge), the management of the whole curriculum (Marland) and the need for training and support for staff (O'Sullivan).

Bearing in mind that it is almost 25 years since the publication of Marland's book and 13 years since that of Bell and Maher, a new book which takes a comprehensive look at pastoral management would seem to be appropriate. Given the dramatic and far-reaching changes which have taken place in the wake of the Education Reform Act of 1988, such a book is overdue. Mike Calvert and Jenny Henderson have done us an important service by putting together such a useful book at this particular time.

Amongst the developments to which the contributors respond are the advent of OFSTED and its cycle of school inspections, the greater financial accountability associated with the local management of schools (LMS), the requirements of curriculum planning in the age of the National Curriculum and the emphasis upon improving, and being accountable for, children's levels of achievement across the subjects of the whole curriculum. The book is thus realistic in recognizing the challenges now faced by an education system which is more and more open to critical scrutiny and (often destructive) public criticism.

The contributors also recognize that schools' responses to these challenges must be purposeful: purposeful in finding effective and efficient means for satisfying the demands of those to whom they are now publicly accountable, and purposeful in identifying and pursuing in a systematic way the goals and values for which good schools stand. This can entail a welcome hard-headedness, as it does in Peter Downes' chapter on resourcing pastoral care where we are reminded that, however altruistic individual teachers' caring might be, institutionalized care doesn't come free. Schools need to cost it and evaluate the efficiency of their provision. There is realism also in recognizing the real benefits that can come from the judicious use of data from OFSTED inspections, uncaring and oppressive as these may seem at the time (see Chapter 7). And there is room for more purposeful self-evaluation as John Scaife shows in his chapter on Interpersonal Process Recall (IPR).

The need to manage change is a recurring theme throughout, and receives explicit attention in Chapter 8. One change in particular – that in the emphasis placed on pastoral care as a facilitator and support for children's learning – is one of the most striking themes in this book. There is nothing caring about allowing children to work to standards below those of which they are capable. Nor is an overweening desire to protect children from the real limitations in their performance an unqualified good thing, however well-intentioned it might be. As Megahy's chapter makes clear, pastoral care must support children's learning; but it must do so in ways which blend challenge with help, compassion with realism, removing or ameliorating blocks to learning and enhancing self-esteem in the process. To use Bernard Harrison's phrase (see Chapter 1), this is all part of the school's management task of 'taking responsibility for people'.

There is, however, a timely reminder that not everything has changed. Some perennials in good pastoral management – the need for schools to locate their caring in the context of inter-agency support (Chapter 5), the importance of 'caring for the carers' (Chapter 3) and the issue of gender (although with a new slant on masculinity) in Chapter 4 – receive a welcome reappraisal.

At a time when target-setting and performance indicators are given high priority, a book which deals with pastoral care as something requiring a planned and purposeful approach is an important addition to the series. The fact that it is underpinned by a fundamental vision of education as a moral endeavour, aimed at the human development in its widest sense, makes it even more so.

Ron Best
Peter Lang

REFERENCES

Bell, L. and Maher, P. (1986) *Leading a Pastoral Team*. Oxford: Blackwell.

Best, R., Lang, P., Lodge, C. and Watkins, C. (1995) *Pastoral Care and Personal-Social Education: Entitlement and Provision*. London: Cassell.

Best, R., Ribbins, P., Jarvis, C. and Oddy, D. (1983) *Education and Care*. London: Heinemann.

Blackburn, K. (1975) *The Tutor*. London: Heinemann.

Blackburn, K. (1986) *Head of House, Head of Year*. London: Heinemann.

Holmes, G. (1993) *Essential School Leadership*. London: Kogan Page.

Marland, M. (1974) *Pastoral Care*. London: Heinemann.

Power, S. (1996) *The Pastoral and the Academic*. London: Cassell.

Notes on contributors

Mike Calvert and **Jenny Henderson** are lecturers in education in the Division of Education, University of Sheffield. Their current writing and research are on the subjects of staff development, pastoral care and management.

Peter Downes is an educational consultant specializing in financial management, educational publishing, school organization and parent/governor/school relations. Until Christmas 1996 he was Head of Hinchingbrooke School, Cambridgeshire, a post he held for 14 years, and where he pioneered Local Financial Management. He was President of the Secondary Heads Association, 1994–95.

Geoff Evans taught in a number of schools before taking up his present post within an LEA. He works closely with schools and parents and is an experienced counsellor and trainer. He is currently working on a community-wide initiative designed to improve provision for young people in an underprivileged urban area.

Carol Hall is a lecturer in Interpersonal Skills for Management at the Centre for the Study of Human Relations in the School of Education, the University of Nottingham. She is currently Deputy Head of the School, with responsibility for development. She has worked as a teacher, lecturer and educational consultant with schools, LEAs and other organizations on aspects of human relations training. She has written and researched in the areas of human relations, training and management, including *Human Relations in Education* (Routledge, 1988), *Scripted Fantasy in the Classroom* (Routledge, 1990) and *Leadership and Curriculum in the Primary School* (Paul Chapman, 1993). Her areas of interest are in organizational effectiveness, integrating personal and professional development and interpersonal skills training.

Bernard T. Harrison is Professor and Dean of the Education Faculty, Edith Cowan University, having held similar posts in the University of Sheffield. His recent books include *The Literate Imagination* (1994) and, with Judith Bell, *Vision and Values in Managing Education* (1995).

Tom Megahy is the headteacher of The Elmhirst School, Barnsley, and his previous posts include Head of PSE and Advisory Teacher. Having earlier undertaken an action research MEd in Curriculum and Pedagogy, he has recently completed an MBA, researching into the link between school aims and development planning.

Jon Scaife is a lecturer in education at the Division of Education, University of Sheffield, where for several years he has co-ordinated the Educational and Professional Studies component of the PGCE course. He previously worked in secondary and tertiary education in Leicester. For a long time he has been inquisitive about how people learn.

Alan Skelton is a lecturer in education at the Division of Education, University of Sheffield. He is interested in gender issues and pastoral care (particularly issues around masculinity) and pastoral care for staff in schools and higher education.

Anne Taylor is Assistant Director of Education with Doncaster LEA. She has been president of the National Association of Careers and Guidance Teachers and is on the Executive Council of the National Advisory Council and Educational Guidance. She is a Registered Inspector with OFSTED.

Brian Wilcox is an Honorary Professorial Fellow in Education at the University of Sheffield. He was previously Chief Advisor for the City of Sheffield Education Department. He is the author, with John Gray, of *Inspecting Schools: Holding Schools to Account and Helping Schools to Improve* (Open University Press, 1996).

Introduction

Mike Calvert and Jenny Henderson

In *Pastoral Care and Personal-Social Education* (Best *et al.*, 1995, intro., p. xiv), an early book in this Cassell series, the authors have the temerity to pose the question 'Why bother with this book?' In answer to their question they refer to the changes that have taken place in response to the Education Reform Act and subsequent legislation and the need to 'reclaim some of the agenda'. We believe that headteachers and pastoral managers can, and arguably should, reclaim some of the agenda. Much has happened since Bell and Maher's (1986) book entitled *Leading a Pastoral Team*. Since then, the educational landscape has changed dramatically, in places unrecognizably so, and yet many of the issues, problems and challenges remain. A middle manager in a school that had undergone massive changes over a five-year period described their approach to pastoral care as 'chugging along' (Calvert and Henderson, 1995 in Bell and Harrison). Arguably, pastoral provision has been 'chugging along' in many schools faced by unprecedented calls for change.

A BACKGROUND TO PASTORAL CARE IN THE 1990s

The introduction of pastoral care was brought about or accompanied by widespread changes in education and society. Recent years have seen comparable, perhaps more profound, shifts and it is important to take into account the changes that have taken place since 1987. In curricular terms, the introduction of the National Curriculum has had an important effect on schools. It produced pressures on the timetable and has resulted in the marginalization of cross-curricular themes.[1] The focus of the National Curriculum on core and foundation subjects has distracted attention away from the less powerful and often marginal area of pastoral care.

The market economy created by Local Management of Schools (LMS), open enrolment, the introduction of Grant Maintained Schools, the emasculation of Local Education Authorities and reduced funding have produced a number of pressures, particularly on smaller schools where economies of scale are not possible. Teachers complain of having less time, more teaching, larger classes, a greater number of pupils with special educational needs (SEN) and more responsibilities. Teachers have also seen a change in the way they are perceived by society and attempts at de-professionalization (Williams, 1996; Gilroy, 1992). Money for staff development is limited and training needs often correspond to mainstream curricular concerns, e.g. new examinations or reporting procedures. All this can be set against a backdrop of growing concerns about social fragmentation – the breakdown of traditional patterns of family life, a growing disaffection for schooling, severe problems of unemployment and new patterns of employment (part-time working, casualization of labour) (McGuiness, 1989) and a pervasive drug culture.

Such a general analysis needs to be broken down and given more close attention since it is the way in which schools interpret these shifts that might determine how pastoral care will change and develop in the light of them.

The first changes mentioned relate to the curriculum and the changes that might result from the introduction of the National Curriculum. Undoubtedly the pre-Dearing (1993)[2] changes did have an effect and called into question the time allocated to pastoral care. There appears to have been a lack of coherent planning in the mapping of pastoral issues and this has resulted in the cross-curricular themes being dropped. It now remains up to the school to decide what prominence this area receives. Some support for PSE has emerged from the OFSTED (1995) inspection process which includes the teaching of PSE courses in the inspections and has a section in the handbook which specifically focuses on the 'pupils' spiritual, moral, social and cultural development' (p. 88). It points the way in highlighting issues of pupil attitude, the quality of relationships and respect for others. In terms of the curriculum, it mentions key issues and assessment as well as the spiritual, moral and other dimensions. In terms of pastoral care in general, it focuses on the role of the form tutor, on links with parents and the community, and it takes a stand against harassment and bullying. Guidance is also available in the new legislative provision for pastoral care in terms of drugs, health and sex education.

In more general terms, the education system has become much more hard-edged in terms of content, competition and accountability. The financial pressures brought about by LMS and open enrolment have seen some schools overcrowded and others increasing group sizes for reasons of space or economy. Teachers are being expected to take on more teaching and administrative roles and this, allied to the last point, might well militate against developments in classroom methodology. Teachers find that they have less time to prepare materials and to spend on training, less freedom and space in the classroom, and they are being urged to improve the academic performance of their examination classes to maintain and enhance positions in the league tables and, as a result, increase the numbers on roll.

As well as coping with the above changes, teachers have endured, along with other groups 'a culture of abuse against them and other professionals' (McLaughlin, 1991). With eroded salary increases, a move to de-professionalize a, nowadays, almost exclusively graduate-entry profession and frequent attacks in the press, it is difficult to see how teachers can be expected to take on more and, at the same time, feel the self-esteem that one might consider to be a vital aspect of work in pastoral care. On the subject of self-esteem, Woodhead (quoted in *The Times*, 1996) welcomes a campaign to 'weed out "woolly, simplistic or otherwise corrupt" teaching methods' and challenges the 'teaching philosophy of the 1960s which puts self-esteem above achievement and "child-centred learning" ahead of traditional didacticism'. Such an attack by the head of OFSTED is representative of the type of media attack on the educational establishment.

Societal changes have had a number of effects on schools and cause them to re-examine their provision. The role of pastoral care is influenced directly or indirectly by the society in which we live. Society has expectations of schools in terms of the personal qualities that they seek in young adults leaving school; the school for its part is charged with helping young students to make sense of their world and to prepare them to take their place as responsible citizens. Schools have to address, for example, long-term unemployment for some of their school leavers; greater competition for those jobs that are available with a consequent inflation of the qualifications necessary. The reality for many of our young students is generally bleak. Commentators (Hutton, 1996; Hillman and Maden, 1996; Maden, 1996) present a depressing picture of declining standards for many less-advantaged students and a growing rift between the 'haves' and the 'have-nots'. Maden quotes the Joseph Rowntree Foundation report on Income and Wealth (1995) which revealed that 'post-tax weekly income of the poorest tenth of our society has actually fallen by £84, while that of the richest tenth has risen by £557' and that the government's own Households Below Average Income survey (DSS, 1994) reveals that 'it is families with children that have increased as a proportion of those in the poorest groups' (p. 19). The extent of the deprivation is often concentrated in particular areas such as some inner London boroughs and this polarization is seen to be particularly pernicious. Evidence collected by ILEA (Inner London Educational Authority) and published in a *Times* article (1995) revealed that 'a substantial proportion of children face not just one but several disadvantages throughout their childhood and that the impact of such factors is cumulative'.

With the growing recognition of the social inequalities and the problems that beset many young people, it is predictable that schools are being increasingly held accountable and pressure is being brought to bear from a variety of sources: the government, the press, the Inspectorate, QCA and the public in general. Watkins refers to 'moral panics' (1995, p. 132) that influence curriculum content as a response to 'what's the school doing about this?'

Another subtle change is noted by commentators like Tomlinson (1996) who refers to the shift towards a market economy post-1979 which militates against teachers' notions based on all pupils having equal worth. He also notes that the advent of a pluralist society removes a 'lodestar' for teachers, parents and politicians and that schools are the first to be affected. The creation of a moral community in schools is most difficult to achieve.

THE CHALLENGES TO MANAGEMENT

There is no pretending that the challenges to management are straight-forward. The following list (adapted from Calvert and Henderson, 1995) presents a daunting catalogue of issues that managers might face to a greater or lesser degree:

- a *lack of shared understanding and agreement* as to the purposes and nature of pastoral provision;
- the existence of an *academic/pastoral divide* – misunderstanding about the importance of the complementary nature of the two and a lack of recognition of the importance of the contribution of the pastoral (Marland, 1989; Power, 1996);
- a resulting *inferior position of the pastoral curriculum* (and lower status for staff involved) with an over-emphasis on academic results (Ketteringham, 1987);
- pressures of an *overcrowded curriculum* and *reduced funding* (Shaw, 1994);
- *teacher overload* – an increase in workload and expectations (Fullan and Hargreaves, 1992; Hargreaves, 1994);
- the difficulty of encouraging teachers to take on an enhanced pastoral role in a climate in which increased demands are being made on teachers generally and *high levels of stress* reported (Turner, 1996);
- a *lack of pastoral care for staff* under such circumstances (McGuiness, 1989);
- a *lack of commitment and confidence* in the pastoral domain on the part of many teachers (HMI, 1988a);
- a *lack of consensus as to the aims, nature, content, skills and processes of PSE work* (Shaw, 1994);
- a *lack of appreciation as to the value of PSE* on the part of teachers and pupils (Lang, 1983);
- *the ineffective use of available resources* (Blackburn, 1983);
- a *lack of a clear role for management* (Hamblin, 1989) and insufficient regard to the training needs of management, as well as of form teachers and teachers of PSE;
- *inappropriate management structures* for developing pastoral care;
- *difficulties in providing adequate preparation* in initial teacher educa-tion and induction (Calvert and Henderson, 1995);
- *lack of monitoring and evaluation of pastoral work* (Power, 1996) and inadequate evaluation of courses and assessment of pupils (HMI, 1988b);
- a *lack of support for*, and *marginalization of, pastoral care* at a national level (Best *et al.*, 1995).

RECURRENT THEMES

A central theme of this book is the need for what Elliott (1991, p. 62) calls 'professional leadership' rather than a manager of resources. We would agree with Elliott that in a centralized, technocratic educational system 'the traditional authority of the head teacher is transformed into the role of managing resources to achieve prescribed outputs'. The contributors, while mindful of the demands that are being made on the professionals who work in schools, are all in their different ways calling for managers with vision who can articulate that vision to produce and develop a clear-sighted, proactive culture in which pastoral care can flourish.

Stoll and Fink (1996, p. 105) offer two models of management which might helpfully encapsulate what is required, 'transactional leadership' and 'transformational leadership'. The former is described as:

primarily about management of school structure. It involves focusing on purposes of the organisation, developing plans, ensuring task completion, facilitating information flow and working well with the various school groups, particularly teachers.

Stoll and Fink argue that while this style of management ensures effectiveness, in a postmodern climate of change with its 'diversity, complexity, indeterminacy and instability' another element is needed – 'commitment'. They advocate instead 'transformational leadership' which they identify more with school improvement. They describe it in the following terms:

Successful principals exhibit a feel for the change process, engage teacher commitment to a shared vision, and model their cultural beliefs through leadership by example. Transformational leaders not only manage the structure; they purposefully impact the culture to achieve school development.

That vision must have a clear view of what the word 'care' in pastoral care means. Caring for pupils is, among other things, about 'managing their personal and academic development' (Griffiths and Sherman, 1991, pp. 149–50). Their ideas are echoed by Stoll and Fink (1996, p. 192) who reject any 'soppy' notions of loving children but allowing academic failures. Instead they state emphatically that 'caring requires quality work from all pupils'. They state:

Caring teachers expect all pupils to do well; they do what it takes to the best of their abilities to help each pupil achieve. The same principles of caring that engage pupils in their learning apply equally to caring for teachers, for parents, for important ideas, or for organisations like schools.

Caring, then, becomes support for learning – arguably a school's central task – both by improving pupils' 'predispositions for learning' (O'Sullivan, 1995, p. 37) and by monitoring and supporting learning through tutoring.

The explicit link between academic achievement/attainment and pastoral care represents a potentially powerful way of breaking down the academic/pastoral divide. Many schools are looking for ways of raising achievement in their pupils, spurred on by the unfair competition of the league tables. Looking again at the curriculum and the impact of tutoring prompts a new look at how the so-called pastoral and academic might enjoy a degree of symbiosis.

A central challenge in the book is for schools to *manage* rather than *maintain* pastoral care. This is not intended to be an unsympathetic observation. Given the pressures imposed by societal, political and educational change, schools often appear to be coping rather than managing – not just as regards pastoral care – and, given its low status, pastoral care is often left to its own devices. It 'chugs along' rather than being managed strategically.

Changing structures of school management would seem to present an opportunity for pastoral care to break away from the parallel hierarchical structures that have grown up in many schools. The call for flatter management with staff taking on wider roles, and the move to team structures rather than hierarchies, lend themselves to an improved pastoral provision. But, as Lodge (1995) warns us, simply changing the job description is not enough. Co-ordination (including monitoring, evaluating and decision-making) has to be linked to clear structures which enable those functions to be carried out.

The ability of schools to improve their pastoral provision will be determined largely by their capacity to understand the changes that are taking place around them and an ability to bring about necessary change. Since change in schools takes place in classrooms, this means changing the behaviours, practices and attitudes of teachers. A number of chapters address the issues of changing circumstances and the need for changing views.

Linked to notions of management is that of accountability. One of the most striking changes in the educational landscape has been the emergence of systems designed to measure achievement in pupils, staff and schools. The National Curriculum, appraisal and the publication of league tables are but three examples of this shift. Pastoral care has not, as a rule, been accountable and, indeed, its effects defy crude performance indicators and measures of output. There is, however, in the current climate a need to be able to demonstrate effectiveness and a need to use scarce resources wisely. As Megahy states (p. 45):

There is no reason why pastoral managers should be any less subject to the processes of accountability than heads of curriculum areas; accepting responsibility for gathering and analysing both quantitative and qualitative data and devising strategies for improvement.

It is argued that there is a need for both self-evaluation and sensitive external evaluation to ensure good quality provision.

This points the way to the last theme that we would want to highlight, namely the issues of equality and entitlement. Some of the chapters explicitly, and others implicitly, call for these principles to be central to whatever provision is deemed most appropriate. Whether it be the issue of gender, care for staff and pupils, inter-agency support or issues of curricular provision, these two principles must be upheld. A local head, in a school which serves a disadvantaged community, when asked what pastoral care meant for him, stated:

I have a strong belief in equality and entitlement and really with the kind of children I've got, the school is the last free beacon of opportunity. It's the last place they can get quality. They can't get it in health now. They can't get it in a range of fields. They *can* get it in the classroom.

This may be quite a controversial view but not one that can be easily dismissed. Schools are not all equal but it is up to us to provide the best possible support for learning in each and every school.

AN OVERVIEW

Bernard Harrison takes up the theme of linking care with support for achievement and argues strongly for whole-school planning which seeks to abolish the segregation of the academic and pastoral 'which can harm the quality both of pastoral provision and also of academic provision, since the quality of one depends so much on the quality of the other' (p. 17).

This holistic approach to pastoral provision is broad, embracing home and community and other stakeholders. His theme is one of breaking down barriers to achieve a more unifying, effective provision. He touches on a number of subjects that are taken up in later chapters and provides a sound theoretical basis for such future treatment.

Tom Megahy is a head with strong views about what schools are for and leaves us in no doubt as to the value and purpose of pastoral care, as the title of his chapter spells out clearly. His quote from Hamblin (1981) reminds us that the call for a link between attainment and pastoral care is not by any means new but that it has not been clearly articulated and understood in schools. His clarity of vision and incisive comments help to set the tone of the book which is designed to continue the tradition of a combined 'literature of technique' and 'literature of critique' that Lang (1995, p. xii) describes. Megahy sets out to present the challenges for pastoral care and highlights the unevenness and lack of clarity in planning and provision. He presents strong arguments for focusing pastoral care on achievement and learning but not without recognizing the caring role. His research, which offers an up-to-date snapshot of pastoral care systems across four Local Education Authorities (LEAs), illustrates clearly that thinking and practice have not moved on in many schools and his findings confirm some of his worst fears. He emphasizes the contribution that the tutoring process can make to 'enhance student learning and achievement'.

In the second part of his chapter, Megahy develops his ideas further and suggests mechanisms for implementing change and realizing goals. He uses management theory to inform his own practice and, like Downes, can demonstrate how the ideas have been put into practice in his own school. He rejects 'bolt-on' solutions and can demonstrate through his initiatives his commitment to whole-school planning. He feels it is essential that 'schools develop a shared vision regarding the nature of the teaching and learning experience they wish to offer'. He returns to the theme of learning, where his analysis of the allocation of responsibility points leads him to conclude 'that, in many schools, large numbers of personnel and significant financial resources are being poured into an area whose purpose is at best unclear, and has little direct relationship with the organization's primary learning objective'. While Griffiths and

Sherman (1991, p. 149) assert that 'growth and development – personal, social and academic – is the main purpose of education and specifically of pastoral care', Megahy persuasively argues for learning to be the school's primary purpose.

Chapters 3 and 4 by Carol Hall and Alan Skelton, respectively, take us away from the structures and procedures that are dealt with in earlier chapters. That is not to say that the concerns they raise are in any way peripheral. Both would argue that the issues of pastoral care for staff and the role of gender in schools are not refinements for those well-funded schools with everything in place but are essential for the well-being of all pupils and teachers.

In the first of these two chapters, Carol Hall underlines the need for staff to be 'fit for purpose', i.e. having the physical, emotional and psychological strength to be able to cope with pupils' problems and for them to have the degree of self-knowledge, self-esteem and self-worth that enables them to deal with the challenges. On one level, the chapter is essentially about self-management, since we must all take responsibility for ourselves. But, beyond this, Hall is arguing that management has a duty to support staff in this domain and to set up systems which enable staff to share their feelings and frustrations and off-load some of the problems that pupils present them with. Hall invites us through a number of short activities to explore our current state through a series of direct questions or statements. Each of the activities could well be used on staff development days as a means of addressing the issues. Hall is not alone in emphasizing 'care of staff'. Griffiths and Sherman (1991, p. 150) end their book with the statement that:

It is our firm belief that the care of staff, by management and by each other, is not just an end in itself, worthy though that end may be, but the basis and necessary foundation for the school's task of caring for its pupils.

Alan Skelton's arguments echo Hall's in so far as the needs of staff are concerned and stress the importance of applying notions of pastoral care to staff as well as pupils. His chapter is framed by three crucial questions which address the problem of masculinity in schools: 'what a pastoral curriculum might include, how it is to be organized and who will take responsibility for its co-ordination'. He argues that a carefully managed programme which addresses these issues can promote positive behaviour in boys. He presents a gloomy picture of what he describes as the 'crisis of masculinity' and describes some of the societal shifts that have led to changes in male behaviour. He draws our attention to the need for gender being regarded, like pastoral care, as a whole-school issue. He reminds us that in the 1970s and 1980s, gender work in school focused on empowering women and that this should be supplemented by an approach which takes into account the needs and experiences of men and allows them to explore their emerging feelings and opinions. He challenges the 'inappropriate business model' of management involving competition, hierarchy, finance and inspection which he sees as being far removed from what pastoral care seeks to achieve, namely a caring community, concerned with people.

Both Hall and Skelton see one of the roles of pastoral middle managers as that of advocate. For this to happen, they need to have the training and understanding to address the issues and help others to both understand them and act upon them. Both writers present a considerable challenge to management but one that arguably cannot be ignored.

Calvert, Evans and Henderson look at the challenge of multi-agency co-operation. By focusing on two urban schools in areas of social disadvantage, they highlight the tensions and pressures on schools and other agencies to work in the child's best interests. They argue that in terms of special needs, child protection, exclusions and health related issues, schools carry heavy legal and moral responsibilities. These call for good systems of communication, harmonization (where possible) of procedures, record-keeping, agendas and training and a greater understanding by staff of what the agencies do and what they need to know.

Peter Downes who, until Christmas 1996, was head of one of the largest comprehensive schools in England, gives a characteristically 'hard-headed' (but not hardhearted) analysis of the costs of pastoral care. Peter Downes is well known for his work on budgeting (Downes, 1993) and a key theme which runs through his work is the importance of appropriate information being available to inform the decision-making process. He suggests ways of using time more profitably; using non-teaching staff, new technologies and using teachers' time more productively. Downes justifies the 'expensive model' of pastoral care in his school and is able to demonstrate that the funding has been worked out equitably. It is interesting to note, for example, the fact that in his school, Personal and Social Education (PSE) was given the same resource allocation *pro rata* as other subjects of a similar kind. In how many schools can that be said to be the case? He echoes Megahy's claim that pastoral care should primarily be about 'helping children learn effectively'.

Anne Taylor and Brian Wilcox address the subject of inspections in Chapter 7. Anne Taylor is a registered inspector and Brian Wilcox, prior to his work researching in this field (Wilcox, 1992; Wilcox and Gray, 1996), was Chief Education Officer for Sheffield. They begin by examining the new 'instruments' (OFSTED, 1995) and illustrate the dangers of the provision appearing to be 'fragmented and lacking in coherence'. They offer practical advice to managers in preparing for inspections and suggest ways that the process and the information generated can be used to sharpen the focus of pastoral provision giving pointers to improved practice. They underline the need for schools to present their pastoral provision as 'a distinct aspect; presented as a clear statement of policy and practice'. They suggest that the published reports themselves can be used for highlighting aspects of good practice which can then be adopted. The inspection process will be mainly of interest to UK readers but the notion of external evaluation of such a broad area of school life poses interesting issues for all.

Meeting the changing demands on schools calls for the implementation of new practices and approaches. Mike Calvert draws on his research into managing change in pastoral care to examine a number of issues involved in bringing about change. He begins by setting the scene in terms of the demands that have been placed on the teaching profession and the consequent reluctance on the part of teachers to take on even more work or responsibility. He then identifies some of the factors that make managing change in this sphere arguably different from that of other areas of the curriculum. He presents a structural framework in which change might be brought about and highlights key areas. He illustrates the many pitfalls and urges managers to spend much more time on planning before they act.

Echoing Hall's contribution earlier in the book, Calvert stresses the affective dimension to teachers' work. He argues that the changes must be perceived in terms of the individual's personal and professional development as well as satisfying institutional goals. Failure to consider the affective aspects of change has undermined many initiatives (Loucks-Horsley and Stiegelbauer, 1991).

Jon Scaife focuses on a particular approach to staff development which has a significant contribution to make in terms of pastoral care. Interpersonal Process Recall (IPR) offers the opportunity for carrying out detailed, self-directed exploration of interpersonal interactions. Using video or audio recordings made in school, teachers can use IPR to improve their understanding of classroom and pastoral relationships and processes. By focusing on relationships, IPR can have a strong resonance for teachers of PSE which, arguably, calls for a special type of relationship in the classroom in comparison with some other subjects in the curriculum.

It would be a mistake to think, however, that the chapter is nothing other than a description of the IPR method. It is worth noting the culture in which IPR is allowed to flourish and the skills of management in providing teachers with the time and space to experiment and develop according to their own professional interests and concerns. So much in-service training has been narrowly directed at the latest educational[3] innovations, it is refreshing to see an example which is directed towards personal and professional development.

The book ends with a view of how the manager of pastoral care might approach provision in the next decade, and indeed, the next millennium. It seeks to identify the trends and how pastoral care might strengthen its position in school. It reiterates the need for a clear vision, attainable goals, flexible structures and committed individuals who understand and share the commitment towards such a central educational task: that of supporting the personal, social and educational development of our pupils.

NOTES

1. The National Curriculum Council originally included cross-curricular themes in their non-statutory guidance. There were originally five themes: economic and industrial understanding, careers education and guidance, health education, education for citizenship and environmental education (National Curriculum Council, 1990).

2. The government ordered a review of the National Curriculum. This was conducted by Sir Ron Dearing. His proposals, immediately accepted, were for a 'period of greater stability, for the excessive prescription of the National Curriculum to be reduced, and a revised approach to assessment' (Best *et al.*, 1995).

3. An example of this was the 'cascade' model of training that was implemented when the GCSE examinations were introduced in 1988. A small group of trainers 'cascaded' to a larger group who then, in turn, passed on what they had learnt to their schools/departments.

REFERENCES

Bell, J. and Harrison, B. T. (eds) (1995) *Vision and Values in Managing Education: Successful Leadership Principles and Practice*. London: Fulton.

Bell, L. and Maher, P. (1986) *Leading a Pastoral Team*. Oxford: Blackwell.

Best, R., Lang, P., Lodge, C. and Watkins, C. (eds) (1995) *Pastoral Care and Personal-Social Education: Entitlement and Provision*. London: Cassell.

Blackburn, K. (1975) *The Tutor*. London: Heinemann.

Blackburn, K. (1983) The pastoral head: a developing role. *Pastoral Care in Education*, **1**, 18–24.

Calvert, M. and Henderson, J. (1995) Leading the team: managing pastoral care in a secondary setting. In Bell, J. and Harrison, B. T. (eds) *Vision and Values in Managing Education: Successful Leadership Principles and Practice*. London: Fulton.

Dearing, R. (1993) *The National Curriculum and Its Assessment: An Interim Report*. London: NCC and SEAC.

Department of Social Security (DSS) (1994) *Households Below Average Income: 1979–1991–2*. London: HMSO.

Downes, P. (1993) Costing the curriculum. In Preedy, M. (ed.) *Managing the Effective School*. London: Paul Chapman Publishing.

Elliott, J. (1991) *Action Research for Educational Change*. Milton Keynes: Open University Press.

Fullan, M. and Hargreaves, A. (1992) *What's Worth Fighting for in Your School?* Buckingham: Open University Press/Ontario Public Schoolteachers' Federation.

Gilroy, D. P. (1992) The professional rape of initial teacher education in England and Wales. *Journal of Education for Teaching*, **18**(1), 5–21.

Griffiths, P. and Sherman, K. (1991) *The Form Tutor: New Approaches to Tutoring in the 1990s*. Oxford: Blackwell.

Hamblin, D. (1981) *The Problems and Practice of Pastoral Care*. Oxford: Blackwell.

Hamblin, D. (1989) *Staff Development for Pastoral Care*. Oxford: Blackwell.

Hargreaves, A. (1994) *Changing Teachers, Changing Times*. London: Cassell.

Her Majesty's Inspectorate (HMI) (1988a) *The New Tutor in School*. London: HMSO.

Her Majesty's Inspectorate (HMI) (1988b) *A Survey of Personal and Social Education Courses in Some Secondary Schools*. London: DES/RMSO.

Hillman, J. and Maden, M. (1996) (eds) Lessons in success in the National Commission on Education. In *Success Against the Odds*. London: Routledge.

Hutton, W. (1996) *The State We're In*. London: Vintage.

Joseph Rowntree Foundation (1995) *Income and Wealth*. York: Joseph Rowntree Foundation.

Ketteringham, J. (1987) Pupils' perceptions of the role of form tutor. *Pastoral Care in Education*, **5**(3), 206–17.

Lang, P. (1983) How pupils see it: looking at how pupils perceive pastoral care. *Pastoral Care in Education*, **1**(3), 164–75.

Lang, P. (1995) Introduction. In Best, R. *et al.* (eds) *Pastoral Care and Personal-Social Education: Entitlement and Provision*. London: Cassell.

Lodge, C. (1995) School management for pastoral care and PSE. In Best, R. *et al.* (eds) *Pastoral Care and Personal-Social Education: Entitlement and Provision*. London: Cassell.

Loucks-Horsley, S. and Stiegelbauer, S. (1991) Using knowledge of change to guide staff development. In Lieberman, A. and Miller, L. (eds) *Staff Development for Education in the '90s: New Demands, New Realities, New Perspectives*. New York: Teachers College, Columbia University.

McGuiness, J. (1989) *A Whole-School Approach to Pastoral Care*. London: Kogan Page.

McLaughlin, M. W. (1991) Enabling professional development: what have we learned? In Lieberman, A. and Miller, L. (eds) *Staff Development for the '90s: New Demands, New Realities, New Perspectives*. New York: Teachers College Press, Columbia University.

Maden, M. (1996) *Greenwich–TES Annual Education Lecture, 1996: Divided Cities: Dwellers in Different Zones, Inhabitants of Different Planets*. London: Greenwich/TES.

Marland, M. (1989) *The Tutor and the Tutor Group*. London: Longman.

National Curriculum Council (1990) *Curriculum Guidance 3: The Whole Curriculum*. York: National Curriculum Council.

OFSTED (1995) *Guidance on the Inspection of Secondary Schools*. London: HMSO.

O'Sullivan, F. (1995) Training and support for pastoral care. In Best, R. *et al.* (eds) *Pastoral Care and Personal-Social Education: Entitlement and Provision*. London: Cassell.

Power, S. (1996) *The Pastoral and the Academic: Conflict and Contradiction in the Curriculum*. London: Cassell.

Preedy, M. (1993) *Managing the Effective School*. Milton Keynes: Open University Press.

Shaw, M. (1994) Current issues in pastoral management. *Pastoral Care in Education*, **12**(4), 37–41.

Stoll, L. and Fink, D. (1996) *Changing Our Schools*. Buckingham: Open University Press.

Tomlinson, J. (1996) Lecture at the Queen's University, Belfast on 21 May 1996.

Turner, R. (1996) Stress in the secondary school: a management strategy for reducing stress among staff. *Pastoral Care in Education*, **14**(3), 3–5.

Watkins, C. (1995) Personal-social education and the whole curriculum. In Best, R. *et al.* (eds) *Pastoral Care and Personal-Social Education: Entitlement and Provision*. London: Cassell.

Wilcox, B. (1992) *Time-Constrained Evaluation*. London: Routledge.

Wilcox, B. and Gray, J. (1996) *Inspecting Schools: Holding Schools to Account and Helping Schools to Improve*. Buckingham: Open University Press.

Williams, B. (1996) *Freedom on Probation*. London: AUT.

CHAPTER 1

Managing pastoral care in schools: taking responsibility for people

Bernard T. Harrison

Reflecting on school changes that she had witnessed, between the 1970s and 1990s, a headteacher commented:

When I began my teaching career, we would gently mock our Head (but not to her face) when she made solemn remarks about the pupils being a 'precious cargo'. But we also believed her. I am afraid, though, that we have been tempted in recent years, to see pupils increasingly as resource units, whose success or failure in examinations reflects well or badly on the school and the staff. Without losing the gains that we have made, we must start again to think first about people, both pupils and staff. Then schools might become the worthwhile and civilised places that they should always aim to be. (Ann – headteacher; quoted in Harrison, forthcoming).

In this brief comment, Ann encapsulates two broad educational movements, from the 'caring school' rhetoric of the 1960s and 1970s, to the accountability-and-performance pressures of the 1980s and 1990s. Yet she also predicts a further, already emergent movement, which places renewed emphasis on the actual people who constitute a school. Ann acknowledges that no modern school leader can simply put the clock back, in order to retrieve a commitment to humane values in schools that may or may not have existed in previous times. The phrase that she cites, about learners as a 'precious cargo', may seem quaint to modern educators, given the turbulence of postmodernist conditions in which all organizations, including schools, now operate.

The now well-established enterprise climate is only part of the explanation for this turbulence. Even more radically, the values which underpinned that notion of a 'precious cargo' have been under regular attack since the 1980s. Some educationists and social theorists would argue that there never was a golden time when human values were held in particularly high esteem by schools, at least where respect for the actual experience of school students is concerned. The notion of 'pastoral care' was itself challenged, for example, by Foucault, whose influential critiques of authority extended to the domain of pupil care in schools. Foucault identified Christian-paternalist ethics in the term, and argued that pastoralism employed 'power techniques intended to rule individuals in a continuous and permanent way', through 'examination, confession, guidance and obedience' (McNay, 1994, p. 120).

Yet 'pastoralism' stubbornly refuses to be an obsolete term, even though its best advocates will accept that actual meanings attached by notions of care and authority have changed. In the words of Richard Berlach (1997), pastoralism is a 'comprehensive concept which embraces the whole life of a school, emphasizing the notion of partnership rather than subordination'. The vigour of the movement, over more than 25 years, for systematic pastoral provision in school is evident in, for example, texts such as Best *et al.* (1995) and Power (1996), as well as in the good practice of many schools. Schools continue to be safe places for young people. During school hours they are much less likely to suffer abuse, neglect, traffic accidents, emotional traumas or other dangers, than they risk outside school hours. In a world of flux, good schools maintain enlightened care values. They provide frameworks of protection and support, where students 'have the right to be confronted by respons-ible adults who can provide safe interaction situations' (Roebben, 1996, p. 10).

Of course, schools must also provide more than just a safe environment for learners; they must also provide excitement, challenge and discipline. Learning involves a complex mix of dependence, interdependence and independence, and the nature of the power relations between learner and tutor needs constant revision. While it is interdependence which 'ideally allows us to have our own needs met and also to be able to meet the needs of others', dependent relations are also of short-term value in learning, in providing opportunities for 'engagement' between learner and tutor (Tait, 1997, p. 17). In working to get these complex mixes right, and in finding new meanings for pastoral care, teachers are engaged in the important task of developing a new professionalism for themselves, and for the whole community, which incorporates not only change, but also the moral dimensions of change (Nixon, 1997, p. 88).

CHANGING FRAMEWORKS FOR MANAGING PASTORAL CARE: LINKING CARE WITH SUPPORT FOR ACHIEVEMENT

Ann, the headteacher who was quoted at the beginning of this chapter, indicated that during the 1980s there were increasing pressures – from educators, government, parents and employers – to call schools to account through measuring the effectiveness of school education. By the early 1990s, these pressures resulted in a number of important organizational changes for British schools, in such key areas as the local management of schools, the introduction of a National Curriculum, and in teacher education. Yet, even while these changes were becoming operational, new directions for future change were already emerging, where the focus shifted to accepting that schools will only improve when the quality of life for all those who are part of the school organization also improves.

Good teachers and good schools have, of course, always maintained their belief in people, and have managed to implement inevitable change in their organizations without being deflected from their main educational and humane purposes. Their achievements were built on earlier patterns of pastoral care, which were recorded in such influential studies as the pathfinding work of Marland (1974) and in full critical accounts of pastoral care in action, such as those by Best *et al.* (1980). Richard Pring (1985, p. 132) dwelled on the two now familiar aspects of personal and social education which constitute pastoral education; the first of these offered to guide individual students in their personal growth to maturity, while the second placed an emphasis on community and civic aspects of their progress towards adulthood. Following these, Bell and Maher (1986) identified four stages in the development of pastoral care, which had as their priorities respectively: to provide a *control mechanism*; to meet *individual needs* of pupils; to develop *group activity*; and to devise a *pastoral curriculum*.

However, studies of pastoral care provision in the 1990s have tended to interrogate these established aspects. In particular, writers in the 1990s have emphasized the importance of bringing pastoral concerns into the academic mainstream of school life. Griffiths and Sherman (1991, p. 21), for example, placed an additional emphasis on 'school-related activity', to which pastoral care provision should be linked. Such a view had been formed some years earlier by McGuiness (1982), who had urged that, in order to be effective, academic objectives must take into account the needs of individual learners for a personal education. This argument for an integrated whole school approach to pastoral care and to the academic curriculum gathered momentum through such work as Hailey (1990, p. 23), who showed how subject departments might work in tandem with the pastoral aim of a school, in order to enrich both these crucial aspects of school life.

In up-dating earlier views, Marland (1995, p. 106) advocated nothing less than whole-curriculum planning for pastoral provision, which would link academic with personal and citizenship values; and McGuiness (1995, p. 57) identified essential cross-curricular skills for all learners, which can be developed through a whole school approach. These include interpersonal skills; skills in questioning assumptions; critical thinking; collaborative skills; and the ability to reflect and plan. At the heart of these, McGuiness argues, is the 'concept of the self-valuing individual'. From this 'flow the skills, the approaches to knowledge, the confident, asserting, respecting and open behaviour which emerge in good behaviour'.

Certainly, as Watkins (1990, p. 7) indicated, a whole school perspective on pastoral care 'does not mean it is all delivered through the subjects. It means clarifying what the subjects contribute'. Commenting on this view, Kwok Wan Yee (1995, pp. 16–17) suggested that such a version of pastoral care 'supports not only pupil development but also *pupils' achievements*'. Such an integration of personal and social with academic concerns in the school requires, as writers in the 1990s have increasingly recognized, a clear framework of values. For this reason, Chittenden (1993) examined the crucial influence of a school's culture on all of its pupils. The actual meanings that attach to such terms as justice, community or social responsibility depend greatly on the way actual teachers and others in the school enact these qualities in daily life. In short, the skills of citizenship will be evident in all the daily processes and relationships of the school.

During the real school day of real pupils, there are countless pressures and challenges which can, in one direction, generate a greater energy of commitment in meeting the rigours of school demands – yet which, in another direction, may lead to anxiety and even failure. Rudduck *et al.* (1995) argued that the actual experiences of learners in schools must be taken into full account by any school which is seriously concerned with school improvement. Learners are inescapably meeting increasing expectations of them for higher achievement in schools. Real improvement, however, depends entirely on how those expectations are handled within a particular school climate. Within such a framework of concern for whole school improvement, it is clear that earlier notions of a duality between the quality of academic achievement on the one hand, and personal development of learners on the other, will no longer do. The domain of pastoral care must, like the quest for the improvement itself, permeate the whole life of schools.

Following more than two decades of self-doubt, schools need now to develop a greater confidence in their own authority (not authoritarianism), and in the personal dignity of all staff and students. In the light of this, there would be little to gain, at this point, in adding to the prolonged, often heated and now somewhat sterile debate on the rightness or wrongness, say, of Bernstein's well-worn notions (1977) of two orders of knowledge and of control in the curriculum. Pastoral care involves, as Best (1988) pointed out, a great deal more than applying behaviouristic control over school students. Instead, it is more appropriate to move to what Sally Power (1996, p. 55) has termed the 'increasing sophistication of the professional dimension of pastoral care' in order to close the often injurious gaps that can develop between pastoral and academic dimensions in a school. Commenting on the segregation between academic and pastoral provision in particular school contexts, Power sums up: 'Where the academic is visible, the pastoral is invisible. Where the academic has strong insulation, the pastoral has weak insulation' (p. 60). A school which aims, then, to achieve whole school improvement will seek to end such segregation, which can harm the quality both of pastoral provision and also of academic provision, since the quality of one depends so much on the quality of the other.

IDENTIFYING AND MONITORING SUCCESSFUL PRACTICE: INTEGRATING THE CARERS

Integration, moreover, does not just involve in-school pastoral care provision and the school curriculum. Those who are seriously concerned to enhance the quality of pastoral provision in schools know that home–school and school–community links are essential components in achieving good quality pastoral support. This has not always been the case; for example, Clemmett and Pearce (1986) targeted their evaluation techniques for pastoral provision exclusively at school-based staff and pupil perceptions. Teacher and learner experiences remain crucial, of course, in evaluating the quality of pastoral care, but evidence of rich involvement with other key agencies is now seen also as essential. The importance of good home–school links is revealed, not least, through attention to learners' experiences. For example, Tehmina Basit (1996, p. 240) showed, in her study of British Muslim girls, that 'effective home–school liaison is crucial not only for ethnic minority families but also for those indigenous parents who do not come to school'. An inescapable inference of this study is that greater attention must be paid to minority ethnic and religious communities: 'British Muslims and other religious minorities are here to stay and are a potentially important part of the workforce of the future.'

Similarly, early indications from a study in progress in Australia (Harrison *et al.*, 1997) highlight the fact that issues of student school attendance, motivation and achievement must be traced all the way home to family and community attitudes. Parents were identified by Irving (1997, p. 6) as 'essential partners in guidance'. He cited an interesting example of small-scale research which aimed to ascertain parents' views and needs on issues of pastoral provision. In this Leicestershire-based study, parents were asked what the school and parents wanted for their children; how they might best achieve these aims; and what might prevent their achievement. The replies disclosed keen parental interest in a range of social issues – including drugs, bullying, parental/gender expectations and relationships – and discussion of the findings led to further parental–school commitment to examine these topics. Clearly, the monitoring of pastoral care must include the experiences of, and evaluations by, parents and other stakeholders in the school.

On a practical level, the interstices of managing pastoral provision were identified in the 'Umbrella of Caring' that was devised by the West Beechboro School, Western Australia (1996).

A whole-community approach to school pastoral support has the virtue of giving an 'extended family' role to the whole community. This may be of special importance in tackling major social issues such as drugs misuse or child abuse, where the efforts of one agency on its own are likely to have little impact, compared to well co-ordinated policies that involve all agencies.

A notable feature of the West Beechboro model (Figure 1.1) is that this highlights a network rather than a hierarchy of agencies. It is worth emphasizing, at this point (not least, since many schools continue to be highly hierarchical), that many organizations – including previously hierarchical bureaucracies such as the National Health Service – are moving from old hierarchical pyramids to new networking webs. The movement is of special importance to pastoral care provision, given the increasing need to co-ordinate roles of different agencies. In their study of changes in management of the medical profession, Eve and Hodgkin (1997, p. 82) tabulate differences between webs and hierarchies.

Schools that are already moving from hierarchies into webs will have experienced that the advantages of this can exceed attendant risks (for example, of temporary instabilities, loss of direct operational control by the principal or headteacher, and the need to redefine 'redundancy' in terms of task). Yet Eve and Hodgkin acknowledge, too, that the move to webs 'is stressful for professionals' (p. 83). As with doctors, so with

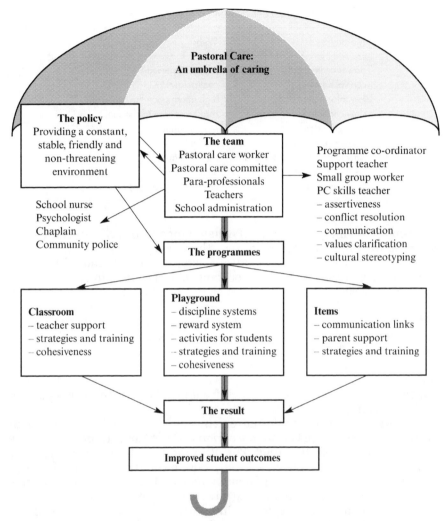

Figure 1.1

pastoral care providers: the move to 'multiple goals' (managing co-ordination with other agencies; promoting successful in-school pro-grammes; balancing resources for pastoral care against other demands) is in tension with more traditional professional aims (where the main task is to deliver the curriculum, and managing pastoral care is someone else's concern). Certainly, webs need to be strong at all points – that is, where all agencies, not just schools, are concerned. Yet schools need to provide essential leadership here, in setting up the web.

THE CULTURE OF CARE: THE CULTURE OF LEARNING

The presence of a whole-community 'umbrella' to protect a school's pastoral support system makes sense in terms of now established notions

Table 1.1 Differences between webs and hierarchies

Hierarchies	Webs
power centralized	power dispersed
control high	control low
low information flows	high information flows
slow changing	rapid response to change
little redundancy	high redundancy
prone to collapse	resilient
slow learning organizations	rapidly learning organizations
single/few goals	multiple goals
errors stigmatized	error = learning opportunity

of life-long learning. The best of what happens in schools represents continuity of family provision; in turn, the world of work should continue to provide, at best, a good blend of pastoral support and of learning opportunities. Schools have an important role, of course, in ensuring that the work experience which learners encounter during their school years should provide full opportunities for personal and social development. As Waterhouse and Turner (1996, p. 34) indicated, such experience involves the testing of self against reality, and offers transition to the adult working world. Their study of students' views on work experience showed that many of their interviewees emphasized the gaining of personal confidence as an important benefit of work experience: in the words of one student, 'they just expected so much from me. And I think I managed to fulfil everything they expected of me' (p. 35).

As the Investors in People movement has shown, industry and commerce have every reason to be serious about continuing to provide personal support for learning. The RSA/industry-based Campaign for Learning has also acknowledged that, since a country's competitive edge depends on people who are confident, skilled and informed, then industry had better join with education to give people the support they need. Again, the emphasis here is on integrating programmes, through a concern for the whole person: 'our aim is to change the culture – to persuade people that they should care about their personal learning in the same way that we are all gradually learning to care about the environment and our own health' (Christopher Ball, quoted in RSA, 1995). Movements such as these look forward to unprecedented new forms of inter-agency co-ordination, in order to make high quality lifelong learning a reality. For too long, and in too many countries where ten years or more of compulsory schooling has been long established, a resistant 20 per cent or so of the school population has derived little benefit from schooling. We can no longer, therefore, continue to provide merely 'more of the same thing', but must rethink traditional provision, which links the work of schools much more closely with health, social community, commercial and other sectors.

The crucial importance of integrating care within a learning framework is highlighted by Jon Nixon's team, in *Encouraging Learning* (1996, p.

vii). The team proposed a theory of learning, to be modelled on the active 'agency' of the learner: 'we learn when we have a sense of purpose and such motivation is best likely to grow out of our active participation in creating the projects which are to shape ourselves as well as the communities in which we live'. The team examined the bases of learning and devised a tabular summary of individual, interpersonal and public aspects of a culture of learning. These aspects are all components in the 'examined life' of any learner who is growing into full citizenship.

Table 1.2 The layers and bases of learning

| Layers of learning | Bases of learning | | |
	Individual	Interpersonal	Public
Understanding (minds)	Practical reason: the examined life	Expectations: ourselves and others	Values: recognizing difference
Self-creation (selves)	Motivation: agency and identity	Support: encouragement	Justice: rights and responsibilities
Social creation (communities)	Mutuality: identity	Civitas: co-operation	Discourse: conversation

(Source: Nixon et al., 1996, p. 51)

The Nixon team accept that enlightened forms of learning and of citizenship are not easily achieved. They confront, for example, those areas of refusal, truancy and disruption which challenge pastoral and learning frameworks alike. They invoke Lyons and Lowery (1986, p. 331), to demonstrate damaging tensions that may exist between, on the one hand, constructive behaviour that leads to loyalty to a school, and on the other hand, destructive behaviour which leads to neglect and distrust. Such patterns of disaffection must, they argue, be resisted in all areas of school life, which includes all the social and academic intercourse of a school day. Although Lyons and Lowery were specifically pre-occupied with disaffection among urban communities, the patterns that they describe may be just as evident in neglected rural communities – for example, in the mining villages of South Yorkshire, which experienced social decay following extensive pit closures during the 1980s, or among indigenous and other neglected communities in the Australian outback.

Personal, social and academic alienation may not, then, be the direct fault of schools that serve such communities; yet the schools cannot evade a massive challenge, to try to make a difference, as far as they possibly can. Where, for whatever reasons, community support is weak, at local or national levels, radical problems that face learners and schools may need radical solutions. Above all, the challenge will be to seek to ensure that learners can lay some real claim to personal ownership and participation in the curriculum. How, for example, might students and their families in such contexts answer questions such as, does this school:

- listen to the problems of its students, their families and their community?
- have effective programmes to ensure (a) student attendance, and (b) student motivation?
- ensure that students feel physically and emotionally safe in school?
- ensure that all students have at least two trusted members of staff, as well as fellow-students, in whom they can confide?
- have a clear picture of any drugs misuse in the school and community, and have an effective programme against drugs misuse?
- have good links with health and social agencies, community policing, local employers and other bodies?
- have effective programmes on sex education and relationships?
- know when individual students are at risk (for example, through drugs, health problems, crime, depression, family crises), and act on their behalf?
- have fair and effective equity policies (gender, ethnic, social)?
- incorporate the above issues in its curriculum?

It is possible that schools whose students and families are answering 'no' to many of these questions, may be tempted to see their students as 'alienated' from school concerns. Yet who are the alienated? Are they those students who find schools to be irrelevant to their needs; or those schools which have failed to make student/family/community links? An Australian Report on alienation in the middle years of schooling identified students at risk as those who consistently:

- feel they can do little to influence their situation at school (*powerlessness*);
- see school as having little relevance to life out of school or after leaving school (*meaninglessness*);
- feel confused by conflicting values and ethos of the school (*normlessness*);
- find little satisfaction or achievement at school (*self-estrangement*);
- cannot engage in the existing teaching/learning processes (*isolation*). (WAFSO, 1995, p. 16, adapted)

What can be done on behalf of such students? Reasonably enough, the WAFSO report emphasized what should be done to improve the curriculum, since that is where schools and teachers have most power to make an impact. The report highlighted that students in the middle years (Years 6–9) have 'unique intellectual, educational, social and personal needs'. It recommended that the organizing and teaching of the curriculum should ensure that:

- students are involved in the planning of what is taught and how it is taught;

- schooling is meaningful to all students in their present lives and their future lives;
- schooling acknowledges individual backgrounds, culture, previous schooling, gender and other equity issues and adapts to the needs of each student in these respects;
- student–student and student–staff relationships are co-operative, inclusive, positive and actively promoted (that is, should work against self/social estrangement);
- all assessment and reporting is based on progress and achievement rather than success/failure and peer comparisons (p. 65).

Some contentious issues are included in these recommendations, most notably concerning the powers of learners to negotiate the curriculum with teachers and communities. These should, however, be seen in terms of a joint quest – among learners, parents, teachers and communities – to get schooling right. It does not mean a regression to a pre-National Curriculum 'secret garden', where schools were not accountable for what they taught. On the contrary, it requires schools to connect with communities. Through doing so, schools can make their distinctive contribution to building learner, parent and community empowerment, on which true teacher empowerment must depend.

Of course, individual learners will continue to suffer individual problems, from which no school policies as such can protect them. These include such traumas as separation and divorce of parents; child abuse; depression and suicide; and bereavement. Of course, schools always face difficult decisions on the allocation of scarce resources; yet few schools and teachers would disagree with Sharon Morgan's view (1994) that these events are far more common than schools and teachers would wish, and that a co-ordinated team approach is needed to ensure that the needs of children in distress are met. Yet, as Adams (1995, p. 172) indicated, 'it is still a widespread public perception that child protection is the job of social service departments'. Schools in England and Wales are, of course, required by OFSTED to have documented policies on such matters as support and guidance for pupils; their social, cultural, spiritual and moral development; and links with parents as well as liaison with other schools (Office for Standards in Education, 1993). However, and as all good schools know, it takes more than policy documentation to ensure that children who are at risk are getting appropriate support at critical times. It is at such times that the quality of co-ordination within a staff team, and then with other agencies in the community, is really put to the test.

Whole school improvement in pastoral care provision aims, then, to break down numerous important barriers – between pastoral and academic frameworks within the school; between those who teach and those who learn; and between the school, its parents and its wider community. Frameworks of pastoral care will continue to be extremely important in all schools. However, we recognize more clearly, now, that – just as no organism or organization can pretend to be an island – the quality of pastoral care must be enhanced and continuously monitored within the wider context of the whole school, and within the umbrella of the whole community.

ACKNOWLEDGEMENTS

The author records, with appreciation, that consultations with Kwok Wan Yee (Singapore) and Richard Berlach (Edith Cowan University) were of value, in preparing this chapter.

The model in Figure 1.1 is used by permission of West Beechboro School, Western Australia.

REFERENCES

Adams, S. (1995) Child protection. In Best, R., Lang, P., Lodge, C. and Watkins, C. (eds) *Pastoral Care and Personal-Social Education*, pp. 171–89. London: Cassell.

Basit, T. (1996) 'I'd hate to be just a housewife': career aspirations of British Muslim girls. *British Journal of Guidance and Counselling*, **24**(2), 227–42.

Bell, L. and Maher, P. (1986) *Leading a Pastoral Team*. Oxford: Blackwell.

Berlach, R. (1997) Unpublished teaching notes. Perth: Edith Cowan University.

Bernstein, B. (1977) *Class, Codes and Control*. Volume 3, 2nd edn. London: Routledge and Kegan Paul.

Best, R. (1988) Care and control – are we getting it right? *Pastoral Care in Education*, **6**(2), 2–9.

Best, R., Jarvis, C. and Ribbins, P. (eds) (1980) *Perspectives on Pastoral Care*. London: Heinemann Educational.

Best, R., Lang, P., Lodge, C. and Watkins, C. (eds) (1995) *Pastoral Care and Personal-Social Education*. London: Cassell.

Chittenden, A. (1993) How can a pastoral care programme improve a school culture? *Pastoral Care in Education*, **11**(3), 29–35.

Clemmett, A. J. and Pearce, J. S. (1986) *The Evaluation of Pastoral Care*. Oxford: Blackwell.

Eve, R. and Hodgkin, P. (1997) Professionalism and medicine. In Broadbent, J., Dietrich, M. and Roberts, J. (eds) *The End of the Professions*, pp. 69–85. London: Routledge.

Griffiths, P. and Sherman, K. (1991) *The Form Tutor: New Approaches to Tutoring in the 1990s*. Oxford: Blackwell.

Hailey, E. (1990) Introducing a whole-school PSG programme. *Pastoral Care in Education*, **8**(2), 19–25.

Harrison, B. T. (forthcoming) See ourselves as others see us. In Bell, J. and Harrison, B. T. *People, People, People: Reflections on the Human Costs and Rewards of Leading Change in Education*. Buckingham: Open University Press.

Harrison, B. T., Wyatt, K. and Partington, G. (in progress) *School Retention, Motivation and Achievement amongst Adolescent Aboriginal Students: An Enquiry into Successful Practice*. Collaborative Study, Edith Cowan University/ Education Department of Western Australia, funded by Australian Research Council/EDWA.

Irving, B. (1997) Parental participation: essential partners in guidance. *Pastoral Care in Education*, **15**(1), 6–9.

Kwok Wan Yee (1995) Staff and student perceptions of pastoral care, and the implications for staff development. Unpublished MEd thesis, Division of Education, University of Sheffield.

Lyons, W. E. and Lowery, D. (1986) The organisation of political space and citizen responses to dissatisfaction in urban communities: an integration model. *Journal of Politics*, **48**(2), 321–46.

McGuiness, J. (1982) *Planned Pastoral Care: A Guide for Teachers*. London: McGraw.

McGuiness, J. (1995) Personal and social education: pupil behaviour. In Best, R., Lang, P., Lodge, C. and Watkins, C. (eds) *Pastoral Care and Personal-Social Education*, pp. 51–8. London: Cassell.

McNay, L. (1994) *Foucault: A Critical Introduction*. Oxford: Polity Press/ Blackwell.

Marland, M. (1974) *Pastoral Care*. London: Heinemann Educational.

Marland, M. (1995) The whole curriculum. In Best, R., Lang, P., Lodge, C. and Watkins, C. (eds) *Pastoral Care and Personal-Social Education*, pp. 105–17. London: Cassell.

Morgan, S. (1994) *At Risk Youth in Crises: A Team Approach in the School*. 2nd edn. Austin, TX: Pro-Ed.

Nixon, J. (1997) Professionalism within the academic workplace. In Broadbent, J., Dietrich, M. and Roberts, J. (eds) *The End of the Professional? The Restructuring of Professional Work*, pp. 86–103. London: Routledge.

Nixon, J., Martin, J., McKeown, P. and Ranson, S. (1996) *Encouraging Learning: Towards a Theory of the Learning School*. Buckingham: Open University Press.

Office for Standards in Education (OFSTED) (1993) *Handbook for the Inspection of Schools*. London: OFSTED/DfE.

Power, S. (1996) *The Pastoral and the Academic: Conflict and Contradiction in the Curriculum*. London: Cassell.

Pring, R. (1985) Personal development. In Lang, P. and Marland, M. (eds) *New Directions in Pastoral Care*. Oxford: Blackwell.

Roebben, B. (1996) Beyond moralizing rhetoric and postmodern cynicism. Moral education in Western Europe. *Pastoral Care in Education*, **14**(4), 7–10.

Royal Society of Arts (RSA) (1995) *Campaign for Learning*, publicity leaflet. London: RSA.

Rudduck, J., Chaplain, R. and Wallace, G. (eds) (1995) *School Improvement: What Can Pupils Tell Us?* London: David Fulton.

Tait, M. (1997) Dependence: a means or an impediment to growth? *British Journal of Guidance and Counselling*, **25**(1), 17–26.

Waterhouse, S. and Turner, E. (1996) Personal development and the self in work experience. *Pastoral Care in Education*, **14**(3), 32–7.

Watkins, C. (1990) The pastoral agenda at Easter 1990. *Pastoral Care in Education*, **8**(4), 3–9.

West Beechboro School Pastoral Care: An Umbrella of Caring (Policy Statement) (1996) West Beechboro, Western Australia.

Western Australia Field Study Overview (WAFSO) (1995) *Student Alienation during the Middle Years*. Geraldton: Geraldton Regional Community Education Centre Association.

CHAPTER 2

Managing the curriculum: pastoral care as a vehicle for raising student achievement

Tom Megahy

INTRODUCTION

At present there are differences of opinion as to the proper tasks to be set, for all peoples do not agree as to the things that the young ought to learn.

(Aristotle, Book 8 of *The Politics, c.* 350 BC)

The controversy regarding the precise nature of the school curriculum can clearly trace its roots back to the early stages of human civilization. While almost all observers would recognize that the curriculum in any society has to adjust to other kinds of social and economic change, fierce debate continues as to the extent to which the curriculum is primarily a means of transmitting knowledge, or a vehicle for addressing social and moral dimensions. One of the most significant developments in British secondary schools over the last thirty years has been the expansion of pastoral care, which, more recently, has increasingly impacted on curriculum provision. In the vast majority of these schools, responsibility for delivery in this area has increasingly been formalized into pastoral systems. Detailed arrangements for its provision and the nature of its content vary enormously from one organization to another.

During the past eighteen years as a form tutor, teacher of PSE, head of department, advisory teacher and senior manager I have had considerable opportunities to observe, at first hand, developments in the field of pastoral care; in terms of both in-depth evaluations within individual establishments, and comparative studies across a range of schools. However, at the same time as reviewing the relevant research literature, I felt it was important to be able to present the reader with conclusions based on evidence which accurately reflects an up-to-date picture of current pastoral provision in the state secondary sector. In addition, as a headteacher currently wrestling with a number of change management issues regarding such provision, I was interested as to the extent to which other secondary heads face similar questions. Data have therefore been collected from pastoral managers across a range of schools within separate LEAs.

This chapter is divided into two distinct yet related parts. Section One is primarily concerned with addressing some of the major issues and concerns regarding the nature of pastoral provision within the secondary sector, and examining how such provision could make a greater contribution to raising student achievement. Questions relating to the most appropriate management structures and systems for the delivery of pastoral programmes, within a whole school approach to pastoral care, form the focus for Section Two.

SECTION ONE: THE NATURE OF PASTORAL PROVISION IN SECONDARY SCHOOLS

After establishing a working definition of pastoral care, this section explores a range of research into pastoral provision over the last twenty years and some of the main issues and concerns which have repeatedly been raised. An attempt is made to illuminate the current situation in secondary schools via analysis of recent primary data, and discussion undertaken as to the extent to which this confirms earlier findings. Consideration is then given to the precise conditions which support effective learning and the specific contribution which pastoral care can make, through the tutoring process, to enhancing student achievement.

Defining 'pastoral care'

Best (1995), in describing 'pastoral care' as a distinctly British concept, points out that reaching an agreed definition of pastoral care has proved an extremely difficult task. Despite the considerable volume of literature which has arisen over the past twenty-five years we have achieved little more than a working consensus. For many, the most authoritative definition, and one which I am content to work within, can be found in an HMI report of an inspection in secondary schools, carried out in 1987–88:

Pastoral care is concerned with promoting pupils' personal and social development and fostering positive attitudes: through the quality of teaching and learning; through the nature of relationships amongst pupils, teachers and adults other than teachers; through arrangements for monitoring pupils' overall progress, academic, personal and social; through specific pastoral structures and support systems; and through extra curricular activities and the school ethos. Pastoral care, accordingly, should help a school achieve success. (DES, 1989, p. 3)

Research into pastoral provision – some issues and concerns

In 1997, Best *et al.* highlighted the paucity of critical analysis in the field of pastoral care, which appears to have stimulated a growing body of research. Since that time, investigations have continued to raise a significant number of concerns regarding pastoral programmes, in particular: a lack of consensus as to the aims, purposes and content of provision (Best *et al.*, 1980); a continuing divide between the pastoral and academic domains (Power, 1996); little evidence that pastoral care is supporting the achievement and attainment goals of schools. From the early 1980s onwards a number of researchers have enquired into the provision of pastoral care and personal and social education in secondary schools. Hamblin (1981) observed:

First hand experience during the last ten years has made me increasingly aware of schools where the pastoral system is underfunctioning, or making little direct contribution to the attainment goals of the school. This did not mean that commitment and involvement were absent. To the contrary: those who held pastoral roles were extremely hard working and displayed deep concern for pupils; but they were largely ineffective because their efforts were unbacked by a structured programme of skills-based guidance for success. They saw themselves as solely concerned with the provision of emotional first aid; as a source of support for pupils under stress; as the equivalent of a social worker or welfare officer or even more vaguely as one whose main task was to 'get to know the pupils'. There is nothing improper about these activities. What is wrong is that for these heads of year they constituted their specialist role. (p. 3)

While Hamblin clearly recognized the genuine commitment to young people among many teachers working within this area, many of his concerns revolved around a perceived lack of clarity as to their roles. Such fears were highlighted by a range of researchers throughout the 1980s.

It was evident to Williamson (1980) that most teachers were less happy about their role as tutors than as subject teachers. Many felt themselves to be working in an area which was vague and uncertain and in which the roles they were expected to perform were often ill defined and confusing. Williamson recognized that the role of the tutor was to give support to the academic aspect of the school's work by helping children to make sense of the variety of learning situations that the school offers. However, he argued that rarely in these meetings was the teaching organization brought into question; more usually the tutor exploited the relationship developed with the pupil to divert attention from such a sensitive area. The tutoring process, with some pupils, became one of 'pastoralization' – using the relationship of mutual trust, knowingly or otherwise, to deflect legitimate grievances away from the inadequate types of learning experience which the school is offering. In this way, Williamson argued that pastoral structures actually prop up and conceal the ailing academic work of the teacher and the school:

Whilst it is widely recognised that low achievement and poor motivation in academic terms may originate in personal background problems needing pastoral care, it is less frequently realised that a good curriculum, well taught, may be an essential agent of personal development, and if not provided, the pastoral organisation may be overloaded with what are mainly self imposed problems. (p. 180)

Best *et al.* (1983) described the concerns they discovered among many teachers regarding the pastoral/academic divide, while Raymond (1985) insisted that it was not uncommon to find schools where tutors had no real idea as to the nature of their task apart from the knowledge that they were supposed to carry out certain administrative duties, concluding that 'they operate within a system that has no explicit aims' (p. 2). Gothard and Goodhew (1987) observed that it would be wrong to assume that teachers are in agreement as to what the term pastoral care means, and went on to describe a number of case studies within secondary schools where there was clear division about pastoral aims, with many seeing them as largely relating to discipline and administration. Duncan (1988) recognized the increasing tendency amongst teachers in secondary schools to specialize in either curricular or pastoral matters. In his view, 'this is a pity for logically there should be no pastoral and academic split' (p. 44). McGuiness (1989), in a plea for a whole school approach to pastoral care, felt that there was a real need for schools to hammer out a consensus on their views of academic and pastoral responsibilities. He was adamant that the most important method of giving pastoral care to students and of enhancing their personal growth cannot occur in a parallel pastoral system, but should be delivered through the everyday lessons of the school:

Pastoral care in schools stands or falls on the care with which the curriculum is constructed and monitored. (p. 29)

More recently, Calvert and Henderson (1995) have described a range of complexities and conflicts that can arise in the contemporary pastoral domain in secondary schools. These include:

- A lack of shared understanding as to the purposes and nature of pastoral provision.
- An obvious academic/pastoral divide where the position of the pastoral curriculum is clearly inferior.
- A lack of commitment and confidence in the pastoral domain on the part of many teachers.
- Inappropriate management structures for effective pastoral care.
- Inadequate evaluation of courses and assessment of pupils.
- Inadequate support for pastoral care at a national level.

The authors are insistent on the need for a strong framework to co-ordinate those involved in the different aspects of pastoral care. Maintenance of the traditional division between the pastoral and academic dimensions of the curriculum means that many schools continue to fail to address the *raison d'être* of pastoral care – that of support for learning.

Such conclusions are supported by Power (1996) who found that pastoral care is usually held to be that part of the curriculum which caters for the social and emotional needs of pupils as opposed to the subject-centred side which addresses the academic cognitive dimension. This confirms Ribbins' (1985) view that initially the term pastoral care appears to have been used to categorize any task that did *not* fall within the confines of the academic. A school's pastoral dimension was often constituted in terms of what it was not – and as such it lacked coherence and organizing principles.

Current pastoral provision in secondary schools

(1) Gathering evidence In order to throw some light on the current situation with regard to pastoral provision, evidence was collected from a cross-section of secondary schools. Data were obtained via a postal questionnaire sent out to 55 schools across the North of England. Two specific groups were targeted: headteachers, who were asked a series of factual questions relating to pastoral structures (see Section Two) and

pastoral managers (heads of year/house) who were invited to comment on their perceptions of the pastoral curriculum within their own schools. Completed returns were received from 36 headteachers and 103 pastoral managers drawn from six LEAs. Such a high rate of response to a postal questionnaire was no doubt due, in large part, to the fact that all schools were contacted on at least one occasion by phone. Potential respondents were assured of anonymity and confidentiality at all stages.

Initially, pastoral postholders were asked how they would best describe the content covered within their pastoral curriculum. A quarter of the sample emphasized issues relating to 'health/sex education' with slightly fewer singling out 'careers' work. One in seven managers chose to use the term 'PSE' as an accurate description of their courses. Other issues, such as 'bullying', 'moral and social education' and 'equal opportunities' received support from a number of respondents, while at the same time a significant element chose to emphasize delivery of the 'cross-curricular themes' of the National Curriculum. Areas such as 'law and order', 'road safety' and 'charities' were singled out by individuals or very small numbers.

Interestingly, fewer than 15 per cent of those replying chose to highlight issues relating directly to raising academic performance (e.g. 'reviewing and targeting', 'study skills' and 'individual action planning'). In almost one in ten cases the major focus was revealed to be 'administration', while in two instances I was informed that content was not prescribed! Overall, 57 separate 'topics' were listed, covering a very broad range of content.

When asked to describe the specific skills and knowledge that their pastoral curriculums aimed to promote, a significant proportion responded in terms of knowledge only. Across the whole sample, issues relating to 'health', 'careers' and the 'cross-curricular themes' received greatest support. With specific reference to skills, 'teamwork' was mentioned most often with slightly fewer choosing to highlight 'communication', 'coping with life' and 'decision-making'. However, as with the initial question, the number who chose to single out issues relating specifically to raising academic performance was very low – in this case fewer than 10 per cent. Overall, 47 separate skills or areas of knowledge were listed.

The final question which was asked of pastoral managers related to how they chose to define 'tutoring' in relation to pupils in their school. As might be expected, answers were extremely wide ranging, but for purposes of analysis they might be seen as falling into one of three broad categories. Within the first group (representing just under one-third of respondents) the process of tutoring was viewed overwhelmingly from a reactive viewpoint – the tutor responding to problems/incidents which are brought forward by pupils:

'Overseeing each individual – ensuring they have someone to listen to their problems.'
'Choosing examples of problems for individual, group or class discussion.'
'Overseeing behaviour problems, counselling and listening.'
'Giving help and advice on any issue of concern and helping pupils to overcome any problems they may encounter.'

By far the largest category of responses (over half the sample) could be defined as those which emphasized a caring/welfare role which highlights the non-academic, social and emotional:

'Caring for them. Helping them to develop concern for others.'
In loco parentis. Informing, nagging, listening, caring and comforting.'
'It is concerned with the social and emotional side.'
'Acting as a parent in a very full sense, giving help, care and support.'
'Tutoring in my school is the provision of a team identity, caring oversight, and, when necessary, disciplinary support.'

As with previous questions only a small number of respondents (fewer than 10 per cent) chose to accentuate issues relating specifically to gains in learning and academic performance:

'Ongoing support and guidance regarding academic progress. About raising achievement.'
'Monitoring subject progress.'
'Conducting action planning and review sessions.'
'Monitoring academic progress closely through review and action planning.'

Perhaps the most honest comment overall came from the teacher who said of the tutoring process 'in my school it isn't defined at all, it's in the hands of the form tutors themselves!'

(2) Some thoughts on the current situation   Apart from the responses to the questionnaire, I can draw on my own experiences, in particular a very wide range of conversations with teachers in a large number of secondary schools, undertaken as a head of PSE, advisory teacher and in-service training provider.

The response of pastoral managers to questions on the content and nature of pastoral provision and PSE in their schools, raises some interesting issues regarding curriculum planning in the secondary sector, not least in relation to the fundamental problem of who should deliver and within what framework. The long-running debate as to whether the delivery of PSE should remain the province of specialist teachers or be the responsibility of all form tutors shows little sign of abating. Proponents of the former continue to see major advantages in specialist provision. These teachers have the required knowledge and training, not only in areas of content such as health/sex education, drugs awareness and careers guidance, but also with regard to the methods used in classroom delivery. Their training and expertise enables them to feel confident and comfortable when addressing sensitive issues with young people as they progress through a particularly difficult stage of their lives. Moreover, these staff see the teaching of PSE as their primary role, committing their energies overwhelmingly to the preparation of schemes of work in this area and updating their knowledge on issues which have a tendency to change rapidly.

Increasingly in recent years, however, many schools have moved away from the notion of a PSE department with its own timetabled lessons, to a pastoral programme delivered by form tutors. The prime argument for such a move is that they are the teachers who know their own students best and are, therefore, most aware of the individual needs and level of development of each young person. In light of this, tutors are the most appropriate staff to address sensitive issues with their own forms. At the same time, methods for delivery often place greater emphasis on active and experiential techniques which have the facility to raise levels of student participation and motivation. Teachers are, therefore, able to develop a greater variety of classroom approaches, within an area free from the pressures of National Curriculum assessment or external examination, which can then be transferred to their subject teaching. In this respect, the move away from specialist PSE provision may be viewed as a useful vehicle for extending the repertoire of teaching and learning techniques across the whole curriculum.

The majority of schools within the sample have moved away from specialist provision of PSE. While the reasoning behind such a move may be valid, follow-up conversations with a range of respondents, in addition to my own observations in a number of schools, suggest real concerns among many pastoral managers and others, as to how these developments have been implemented.

There is clear evidence in some schools that the dismantling of separate PSE courses has not been accompanied by a fundamental review of provision across the whole curriculum or clarity regarding the precise nature of pastoral provision. Overworked subject departments have argued that National Curriculum content and assessment overload means that they are unable to give attention to coverage of broader material. In such cases, it is unsurprising that there is resistance to requests for them to take on board additional content, at the same time as pressure to make a greater contribution to the delivery of cross-curricular themes. Subsequently, there is a danger of wholesale 'dumping' of units of work into tutor programmes, with a resultant lack of ownership by tutors, or the commitment of resources to develop the requisite skills for delivery. In schools where this has happened, pastoral programmes become overloaded with issues which are felt to be important, but which apparently cannot be accommodated elsewhere, adding to the lack of a sense of coherence and philosophical rationale felt by many teachers. In addition, such overload squeezes the time available for tutor and student to engage in a dialogue about learning. It is interesting to note that in two schools within the sample, a move has been made to revert to specialist delivery of PSE with an emphasis on content coverage, while retaining additional time with the form teacher to develop academic tutoring.

Specific attempts by respondents to define the process of tutoring also raise real concerns regarding pastoral provision. Evidence suggests that many pastoral managers remain locked into notions of pastoral care reaching back to its etymological roots; promoting visions of the enduring concern of the pastor for his or her flock. Writing at the beginning of the last decade, Buckley (1980) discussed the confusion among many teachers regarding notions of 'care'. Asserting that the relationship between teacher and learner must be right if learning is to happen, the concept of care for a teacher should be the creation of that relationship – 'the teacher who cares is the one who teaches effectively'. It is critical that we understand that development of an ethos where such relationships can flourish in a school is done in order that the processes of teaching and learning can take place effectively, 'not in order that the institution can feel cosy and comfortable'. These concerns can only be compounded by the number of pastoral managers who appear to maintain a reactive approach to pastoral care, viewing provision as essentially a response which teachers make when pupils require support with a problem, usually of a personal, emotional or social nature.

Overall, my research raises some key questions as to the extent to which the provision of pastoral care in a significant proportion of secondary schools has truly developed since the early 1980s. If one accepts that the primary purpose of any organization is to fulfil certain agreed objectives, then in any school this purpose must relate over-whelmingly to *learning* – adding value to the achievement of its pupils.

HMI, quoted earlier, highlighted the importance of the provision of quality teaching and learning in promoting pupils' personal and social development. Does such a philosophy clearly underpin programmes of pastoral care and PSE in many of our schools or is Hamblin's remark of over fifteen years ago still relevant? He observed that many pastoral managers were concerned primarily with providing 'emotional first aid', and in such cases the school's pastoral system was underfunctioning or 'making little contribution to the attainment goals of the school'. It seems that the disquiet expressed around the same time by Williamson, as to whether pastoral care was helping to make sense of, and bring about improvements in, students' learning, remains relevant.

The primacy of learning

A fundamental challenge for schools in delivering effective pastoral care, is how we can support the organization in striving to provide quality learning experiences for all our pupils. Kyriacou (1986) is insistent that the essence of effective teaching lies in the ability of the teacher to set up a learning experience which brings about the desired educational out-comes. If this is to be successful, each pupil has to be engaged in the activity of learning. Before any discussion of the most suitable vehicle for delivering the pastoral programme or its proposed content, it is perhaps appropriate to consider the precise conditions under which learning might best take place. Kyriacou argues that three crucial aspects, which are clearly interrelated, need to be examined: attentiveness, receptive-ness and appropriateness. Attentiveness relates to the ways in which teachers can elicit and maintain high levels of concentration and atten-tion, for example by varying activities and utilizing pupil interest. Receptiveness depends in part on the ways in which teachers can make use of the different sources of pupil motivation to facilitate and encourage learning via such strategies as eliciting curiosity and offering opportun-ities for pupils to succeed. Appropriateness refers to ways in which teachers need to match the learning experience to each pupil's current state of knowledge and understanding, while at the same time ensuring that the desired educational outcomes are being fostered. Effective monitoring of progress and quick corrective feedback, and ensuring the type of questioning used in appropriately assessing the learning required, would usually feature prominently in this process.

Lofthouse (1994) quoting Blyth (1988) reminds us that we should 'always remember that children's learning is more important than teachers' teaching'. We are asked to reflect on how often memories of our own schooling tend to focus on the conditions in which instruction was conducted as opposed to the learning we experienced. In his view, facing confusing and diverse demands it would be fatally easy for senior staff in schools to allow their institutions to serve the needs of the providers (teachers) rather than address the often unexpressed needs of their clients (the learners). This outcome may merely reflect increasing pressures on teachers to be accountable for what and how they teach – a situation intensified by the revised OFSTED Inspection Schedule (OFSTED, 1995) which requires inspection teams to report by name particularly strong or weak teachers. Most definitely the continuing pressure from some quarters for a 'back to basics' approach and return to so-called 'traditional values' lends support to the notion of the teacher as the provider of specific selected information. Consequently, as Lofthouse warns, the role of the learner in such a scenario is one of passivity; being willing or unwilling recipients of teachers' wisdom.

I believe it is crucial that such moves should continue to be resisted, not only in terms of ensuring the development of each pupil, but also in meeting the needs of a society, in the twenty-first century, for flexible highly skilled individuals, with a commitment to, and the ability to undertake, lifelong learning. However, in order to do this effectively we have to address the question as to what kind of pastoral provision can make a significant contribution to enhancing student learning and achievement. At the very heart of the answer, in any secondary school, must be discussion and subsequent clarification of our understanding of the tutoring process.

Tutoring as a process for raising achievement
Waterhouse (1991) has defined tutoring as:

The intensive support given to learners, usually in small groups, which is designed to enhance the quality of their learning. It recognises that learning is a subjective matter and so its role is to nurture, to encourage, and to minister to processes that are already going on within each student. Its repertoire of styles and techniques is a broad one, drawing on the best practice in teaching and counselling. Its long-term goal is the autonomy of the learner. (p. 8)

In his view, the pastoral tutor needs to get involved with the substance of the learning experiences being encountered by pupils; knowing that the pastoral tutor knows about and cares about the current learning tasks can be very reassuring. Marland (1989) lends support to this notion, recognizing that one of the most important aspects of a tutor's role is helping pupils to see how they can make good use of teachers, support staff, resources and the way the school is organized. Central to this concept is assisting teachers to reflect on their experiences in lessons, including the teacher's aims, the methods used and pupils' own learning approaches and successes. This process has to be proactive; deliberate planned input is needed if it is to be successful. However, Marland identifies, quite properly, one important deficiency which must be remedied – the fact that pupils and teachers lack a shared technical language for talking about pedagogy. Part of any effective tutorial programme should be about providing this possibility. When managed successfully, 'the tutor group is also the laboratory of the understanding of learning'.

Griffiths (1995) suggests that the basic principle of all tutorial and guidance work is to help students to 'take increased and increasing responsibility for themselves, for their academic work, for their behaviour and for their actions' (p. 76). Whether the guidance is with individuals or whole classes, by subject teachers or form tutors, and whatever the content and purpose, the aims and principles remain the same.

In his view, two key developments in recent years have pushed tutoring and guidance towards the centre of schools' activities. TVEI, with its insistence on discussion, negotiation and counselling, resulted in an expectation that students would take part in planning and reviewing their own work. At the same time, the introduction of GCSE, with its emphasis on coursework, made similar demands for individual supervision, discussion and negotiation. Griffiths points out that the two activities grew out of, and were reinforced by, other developments: profiling, ROA and pupil-centred/flexible learning. As he rightly observes:

Each of these demanded skills rarely touched on in initial training – the basic skills of tutoring and guidance, or reviewing, negotiating and planning for individuals and of that whole are known as 'listening skills'. (p. 76)

Griffiths argues that the necessary skills for this had originally been acquired and developed by some teachers but now had to be taken on by a far wider range – becoming the responsibility of the majority of staff and not just those within pastoral positions. What were regarded as pastoral skills were being applied directly to further academic work and achievement, with a consequent merging of the pastoral and academic 'sides' of schools and the spread of those skills among all staff. Where this happens the pastoral/academic divide begins to disappear and tutoring and guidance become 'not an academic or pastoral task but a teacher task' (p. 77).

The vast majority of teachers in secondary schools are or have been form tutors, and for around 90 per cent of their time, when not being form tutors, they are teaching their subject. In Griffiths' view it would be absurd to assume that they then become different people with different attitudes, values, experiences, skills and ways of relating to students. Tutoring, therefore, is not something done only by tutors but is an interaction between teachers and students aimed at helping young people take responsibility for themselves.

Munby (1995) adopts the position that perhaps the greatest challenge for any school which attempts to have a whole school approach to pastoral care and PSE, is how to tackle the assessment issue. He believes that ongoing and effective teaching and learning cannot be achieved without a clear strategy for assessment. Because we are rightly concerned about learning rather than just teaching, we need to know how much of what has been taught has been understood by the learners so that we can help them to learn some more. Assessment provides the feedback loop to the teacher – it makes teaching a two-way process.

Among certain key principles of learning centred assessment proposed by Munby are a number of issues which are, in my view, critical to any consideration of effective tutoring:

- We need to be clear about the difference between achievement and attainment and ensure that the assessment recording and reporting of attainment is carried out using an achievement-based approach. We must ensure that students are given opportunities to be involved in their own assessment, and that grades and levels are not reported to parents in isolation. This requires that proper, supportive reviewing procedures are built into the school's tutorial system to help the individual student to make sense of his/her attainment and provide a person-centred context.

- Students should be involved in the assessment process, not only because it is more likely to motivate them as learners or that they should be entitled to involvement, but because, by involving them, it is likely to lead to more accurate judgements about their attainments. As Munby observes:

  It is, I suggest, the grossest form of egotism to think that nothing has happened in your classroom of which you, the classroom teacher, are not aware, and that no additional evidence could possibly be brought to bear by the students that is not already known by you. (p. 145)

  We should be involving students in their own assessment because we are professionals and because we want to ensure that our judgements are accurate.

- Target setting is particularly difficult to implement effectively. High attainers are rarely given truly challenging targets ('keep up the good work') and low attainers are often asked to 'concentrate more' or 'work harder' rather than being given useful and graspable targets. Munby rightly stresses that effective strategies for raising individual achievement often involve the setting or negotiating of challenging, appropriate, specific and achievable targets. Such targets require regular monitoring and review and, if they are to have a positive impact, they need to be communicated effectively and meaningfully to students and parents.

Munby's experience points to the fact that, in spite of the existence of tutorial groups and pastoral care systems, students do not receive coherent and integrated feedback concerning their learning and development at school. Many schools are realizing that, in spite of the time-tabling and human resource costs, one-to-one reviewing between a student and his or her tutor is fundamental. A significant number are coming to the view that a structured reviewing process is a very effective way of monitoring the progress of individual learners and helping to make sure students reach their potential.

Recently we have seen a growth of interest in value added measures as one of the many aspects that inform school improvement. Betterton and

Nash (1996) observe that this interest is not only in the provision of data demonstrating how pupils have increased attainment over a period of time, but also how the form tutor is directly involved in the process of improving students' attainment, through specifically focused interviews and target setting. The model of academic tutoring developed in their LEA consists of a monitoring system of one-to-one tutorials focusing on agreed action plans for improving achievement, with built-in termly reviews. Reliance upon good assessment data from departments demands that subject teachers have to be specific regarding learning progress and targets, using language which can be interpreted by non-specialists. Above all else, in common with other successful academic tutoring schemes, the central aim (enabling pupils to achieve their potential) is in line with the school aims.

The strategies outlined here describe a real attempt to involve pupils actively in their own learning, not merely as a recipient of what has been deemed appropriate, but by participating in a genuine dialogue with teachers who are being forced to consider carefully the ways in which pupils learn in the context of their classrooms. While I would find the prospect of such a process becoming accepted practice in all secondary schools both positive and exciting, we must be conscious of its potential impact in the initial phases of its introduction. As Buckley (1980) has warned:

From such dialogues, gradually and continuously, the contract between teachers and learners may be renegotiated. The readjustment of the traditional relationship between teacher and learner will be accompanied by discomfort, unease, and insecurity on both their parts. The duty of care will remain, but the notions of 'pastoral care' and of 'loco parentis' at the secondary level of education may become less appropriate. (p. 195)

All writers in this section demonstrate significant agreement about the need for a carefully planned and proactive approach to tutoring, whether as part of pastoral provision or in subjects. At the same time, they raise some telling issues which deserve further consideration. Waterhouse (1991) raises the importance of the pastoral tutor having knowledge of the learning task within different subjects. I would question the extent to which such knowledge is common among teachers in the secondary sector (though not within primary schools). If we accept the notion that a broadening of knowledge in different subjects will enhance the tutoring process, there is a clear case for ensuring all teachers develop this. Initial teacher education courses could do much to bring this about, with school based in-service time making a further contribution. Indeed, some of the most exciting and, according to teacher feedback, useful activities I have experienced on school INSET days, have involved staff being given the opportunity to learn about the work of colleagues in other areas and share examples of good practice. Certainly, the introduction of the National Curriculum should make the dissemination task easier and reduce the need to update oneself constantly on changing courses.

Marland emphasizes the need for tutors to support students in giving them the skills to make good use of all learning resources – both human and material. One crucial prerequisite in meeting this objective is developing the ability of young people to understand their own learning needs and be genuinely assertive in seeking solutions. At the same time, it will require some secondary schools to re-examine the nature of the relationship between teachers and students. Marland's appeal for the development of a shared language for discussion about pedagogy is a major step forward in this direction, though there is little evidence as yet of such movement in many schools. Working towards this position needs to become, in my view, a critical feature in all secondary schools when planning pastoral provision.

I find Munby's arguments regarding the importance of assessment as a tool to bring about improvements in teaching and learning particularly compelling in relation to tutoring. While clearly many of his comments are equally applicable to subject teachers, he highlights two key issues which should be at the centre of our pastoral work:

1. He places emphasis on the way in which tutorial review can develop teachers' understanding of what has been learnt and what factors were responsible for this. The pastoral tutor is in a unique position within the school to be able to gain insight into the whole learning experience of her/his tutees and thus be able to build up a more accurate picture of the quality of that experience – including its strengths and weaknesses. Pastoral teams subsequently have the evidence to report back to curriculum areas on ways in which further gains in learning could be made. Responsibility for co-ordinating this process and maintaining liaison should be a major role in the work of secondary pastoral managers.

2. At the same time Munby highlights the importance of involving students in their own assessment. Once more, I feel the pastoral tutor has a crucial synthesizing role to play in this process, helping students to interpret information from a wide variety of subject areas, searching for patterns, identifying areas for consolidation or development and beginning to frame realistic and attainable targets for improvement. Where this is done effectively, not only does it lead to far more coherent and integrated feedback to students, but it has the capacity to initiate a far greater level of meaningful dialogue with parents.

The potential for the tutoring process to make a contribution to value added initiatives, via a formal structured system of reviews, is demonstrated by Betterton and Nash (1996). In addition to highlighting the importance of the pastoral tutor, their model of review also exposes the need for subject teachers to consider more carefully how they give feedback to students. Where this is done successfully, one likely result will be a broadening of subject knowledge among pastoral tutors – the desirability of which has already been discussed.

When one takes into account all the potential developments described here, Griffiths' contention that the key to effective tutoring is helping students to take increasing responsibility, appears sound. At the same time, in attributing importance to TVEI and GCSE in extending the range of teachers with confidence in the areas of planning and review, he accurately describes the effect of such developments within the secondary sector. I do, however, feel bound to inject a note of caution regarding the extent to which this impetus has been maintained, and the level to which it has impacted on pastoral provision in many secondary schools. My concerns fall into two main areas:

1. Increasingly centralized prescription regarding examination courses and their modes of assessment has led to a very significant reduction in the element of coursework allowed. When one adds to this the pressure on departments to deliver results to boost standing in league tables, based on students' performances in terminal examinations, it is perhaps unsurprising that the time teachers feel able to give over to tutoring within their subjects is under pressure. While it is the case, in my own experience, that the most effective departments have reviewed and updated schemes of work in order to retain the benefits of a tutoring approach, such developments are by no means universal.

2. The assumption that techniques practised by teachers within subject classrooms are automatically transferred to their pastoral role is not borne out by my own observations. There may be a variety of reasons for this, not least the insecurity felt by some secondary teachers in stepping outside the discrete area of their training. Perhaps, most significantly, such transferability is impeded by the design and structure of many of our pastoral programmes, where the emphasis remains on the coverage of areas of content, as identified within my research. Where teachers perceive their pastoral role to be primarily concerned with the delivery of another 'subject' as opposed to a process for supporting students in developing autonomy and raising their performance, moves towards effective tutoring are unlikely to be forthcoming.

In returning to consideration of the conditions necessary for learning, as outlined by Kyriacou, one can see how effective pastoral care has the capacity to enhance the learning task with specific reference to the key areas he identifies. The potential impact on 'attentiveness' resulting from the sheer volume of information regarding students' learning which can be fed back to subject areas by the pastoral tutor, is considerable. Where teachers improve their understanding of how students learn and the variety of different learning styles, they are better placed to offer a range of learning activities which raise the level of concentration and attention. In lessons planned in this way, there is a greater likelihood of students being willing to learn and respond, with a resultant increase in motivation. Where this is allied to a structured programme of target setting and review which is co-ordinated and reinforced by the pastoral tutor, students are presented with real opportunities for success. In both these cases, 'receptiveness' should be enhanced.

The co-ordination of information about student learning across all subjects which the pastoral tutor undertakes, can lead to more effective strategies to meet the needs of individuals, thereby making a significant contribution to ensuring 'appropriateness'. Activities can be devised which stretch the learner yet still allow them to achieve success. The crucial connection between self-esteem and achievement, established by White (1991), is dependent on appropriate matching. It is challenge with success which builds self-esteem, whereas success without challenge is likely to leave students feeling discontented and patronized. Effective tutoring can be instrumental in avoiding this pitfall.

The need for coherence

I have never been convinced of the desirability of attempting to prescribe the content of the pastoral curriculum, apart from the fact that this would immediately encounter major practical problems. The power which schools still retain post-Dearing[1] to determine the amount of time given over to study of any particular area, allied to the idiosyncratic nature of courses in other parts of the curriculum and the multiplicity of examination syllabuses in many subjects, convinces me that any attempt at prescription would be a non-starter. What is crucial, is that any programme should be able to demonstrate the contribution it will make to pupil learning, and how precisely the school plans to deliver this.

Nonetheless, this does not mean that serious consideration should not be given to specific content. I would always seek justification for the inclusion of any 'topic' or issue in a pastoral programme, and question whether this is the most appropriate vehicle for coverage. Certainly my own findings regarding the content of the pastoral curriculum in many secondary schools do little to allay my fears in this respect.

My investigation appears to add weight to many of the concerns raised by researchers over the past two decades, which were outlined at the beginning of this section. A lack of coherence with regard to the content of the pastoral curriculum, indicative of a failure to develop any shared vision of, and priorities for, pastoral care, remains an all too familiar pattern in a significant number of our secondary schools. At the same time, there is continuing evidence of the failure of the pastoral system to focus on support for learning and achievement. Clearly, in such organizations, there is a need to look closely at the potential relationship between pastoral provision and school improvement, in an attempt to develop structures to support the school in getting better at meeting its objectives. Traditional management arrangements for delivering pastoral care, developed in a radically different educational climate over two decades ago, may no longer be appropriate. Furthermore, they may well inhibit moves towards a whole school approach to curriculum planning which has the potential to raise achievement and attainment.

SECTION TWO: EFFECTIVE SUPPORT FOR LEARNING: DESIGNING PASTORAL SYSTEMS AND STRUCTURES

The introduction of the National Curriculum, based around traditional academic subjects, has, once more, raised questions concerning the precise status and role of pastoral care and PSE, and the most appropriate structures and systems for their delivery. This section is primarily an attempt to address these concerns. A starting point is a brief review of the legal position with regard to pastoral provision, which can establish the context within which an integrated approach to school aims and development planning can assist in the creation of a whole school curriculum strategy.

Following this, a consideration of a number of historical factors can assist our understanding of the current situation and the extent to which they may continue to act as barriers to change; a debate which is supplemented by analysis of my own research into existing pastoral structures in the secondary sector (outlined in Section One). Suggestions are put forward as to strategies which could be adopted in a move towards a whole school approach to pastoral care, with the focus on support for learning. At the same time, consideration is given to a number of change management issues which are likely to arise in any school attempting to move in this direction.

Pastoral provision: the current legal context

Marland (1995), in his detailed analysis of the legislative implications of the 1988 Education Reform Act (ERA) for pastoral provision and PSE, insists that the Secretary of State has no power to control the pattern of a school's curriculum other than the definition of the National Curriculum components. In addition, the requirement within the Act for a balanced and broadly based curriculum, and in particular the need for schools to 'prepare pupils for the opportunities, responsibilities and experiences of adult life', could be seen as a statement of the central aim of pastoral care. Indeed, as Marland observes:

Not only therefore is the school the centre of power for curriculum planning against national criteria – there is a statutory justification for building pastoral care into the curriculum. (p. 116)

The relationship between aims and planning

While there is certainly a case for a pastoral dimension to the secondary curriculum, ensuring that entitlement to pastoral care is met requires a whole school approach to curriculum planning. For this, schools must clarify their own purposes and priorities before starting to design strategies for implementation. Clearly, 'bolt-on' models of pastoral care resulting from afterthoughts are unlikely to be effective.

In a business context, Bennett (1996) defines planning as:

the deliberate and systematic determination of what to do in the future, in order to fulfil the organisation's mission and meet its objectives, given certain predicted or intended conditions. ... The planning process can begin as soon as the firm's mission and core objectives have been formulated. (p. 281)

The major purpose of development planning in schools is to improve the quality of teaching and learning via the successful management, in particular, of the implementation of change. In relation to this the desirability of a clear relationship between an organization's aims and planning processes is essential and receives broad support in the education field. Hopkins *et al.* (1994) believe that the process of school improvement will be further enhanced where vision building and planning are directly linked to one another, ensuring that development is rooted in the values and expectations of the school community.

It is of central importance that schools develop a shared vision regarding the nature of the teaching and learning experiences they wish to offer, and the contribution which pastoral programmes can make towards success, before undertaking any detailed plans for implementation. Watkins (1995) informs us that, given a National Curriculum composed of subjects, ways of describing the whole curriculum have advanced very little since 1988, a position which we have no reason to be confident will change. With a continuing lack of clear support or guidance from central government, it remains imperative that schools make a commitment to clarifying their own purposes and practices in this area. Whatever the *modus operandi* adopted, this process may well result in the realization that existing thinking and management structures must change if barriers to implementation are to be overcome. However, before any examination of the precise features such change may require, it is necessary to outline the current position in secondary schools, and those factors responsible for it.

Evolving pastoral systems: a recent historical perspective

Bell and Maher (1986) have described four phases, or 'generations', in the evolution of pastoral care in Britain. Initial developments were linked mainly with the growth in population and expansion of comprehensive education in the late 1960s and early 1970s. The major concern at this stage was with the need to control and discipline large numbers of pupils and enable them to feel they had a place in a large organization. A second phase developed from a notion of care based on individual counselling, but even where teachers possessed the requisite skills this resulted in enormous demands on teacher time. In addition, there was a need to find something for the rest of the tutees to do while individuals were being counselled. It was a search for potential solutions to this difficulty which resulted in the development of phase three: Active Tutor Work (ATW). What had therefore begun as an individual activity now became a group-based programme, often taking place in isolation from the rest of the curriculum and reinforcing the idea of the separateness of pastoral activity. The fourth 'generation' can best be understood as a deliberate attempt to break down this artificial isolation of 'caring' from the rest of school life. In proposing the term 'pastoral curriculum' Marland (1980) argued that this is, in fact, a subset of the whole curriculum which deals with the development of the whole person. Thus, by this definition, some elements of the pastoral curriculum could best be approached via the medium of tutorial activity with form tutors, but other elements, quite properly, should be managed by specialist teachers in their subject areas. Marland's paper was one of the most critical developments of the 1980s; moving away from an *ad hoc*, reactive and fragmented approach to pastoral care, to one which recognized the need for whole school curriculum planning.

Evidence from my own practice and research suggests that many of the features outlined by Bell and Maher in describing their first three phases are still present in the secondary sector, and continue to exert a real influence. The emphasis on control and discipline in phase one remains apparent in many schools; not only through the comments of some pastoral managers with regard to their perception of their role, but in systems and revealed practices which indicate that issues of discipline and behaviour management are not primarily the responsibility of curriculum areas. Where this has become embedded in the culture of a school it can prove a major barrier to change, not least in impeding newly appointed pastoral leaders who may wish to adopt a more proactive stance linked to learning and achievement. I feel sure I am not the only headteacher to listen to complaints from year heads regarding the difficulties they face in developing their work in monitoring teaching and learning. Feelings of irritation at being used as some kind of disciplinary 'sink', however, are exacerbated by a perception that some colleagues actually welcome this situation. Hamblin's (1981) observation that 'an apparently well designed structure can conceal self-defeating attitudes, particularly where the pastoral team is inhibited by Heads of Year, etc. who hold limited perceptions of their functions' remains relevant to some schools today. At the same time, as demonstrated in the previous section, a proportion of pastoral managers are committed to a notion of care which involves reacting to an individual's social or emotional problems. It has been my experience that a number of such staff were attracted to their positions precisely by the prospect of undertaking this work.

I believe that group-based ATW style programmes reflecting the third phase of development are still generally representative of pastoral provision in secondary schools today, and this disquiet regarding the separateness of pastoral activity remains valid. Perhaps of greatest concern is the fact that very few secondary schools could genuinely claim to have a coherent pastoral curriculum which could measure up to Marland's criteria – almost two decades after he first outlined his ideas.

Current systems and structures in secondary schools

In recent years, schools have been operating in an ever-changing context, with the introduction of key changes such as LMS, open enrolment and diminishing powers of LEAs. Lodge (1995) suggests that these developments have sometimes been the driving force behind changing staffing structures, including some reduction in the number of posts with specific responsibility for leading pastoral teams. She confirms that there is some evidence of a change to role titles with year co-ordinator/manager or key stage co-ordinator being the most common. However, some of the new titles are just that – with no apparent change in role, or possibility of this happening within the schools as they are.

As part of the investigation mentioned in the previous section, I sought to gather data on current pastoral structures in secondary schools. Specific questions related to the number of responsibility allowances which were allocated to pastoral management, the time allowed for pastoral delivery and the level of involvement of senior management. While responses showed a very mixed picture, it was still possible to identify certain trends.

Secondary schools continue to invest considerable resources in their pastoral systems. Within my own sample there was an average of one responsibility allowance point for every 60 pupils (with a range of 1:39–1:93). The pattern varied enormously from one organization to another, as a selection of the following six schools demonstrates:

Table 2.1

No. of pupils	Total points
1780	25
1470	33
1260	15
950	21
930	10
750	19

A similar diverse picture was evident with regard to the time allocated to pastoral delivery (however the school chose to define this). Responses revealed an average commitment of 100 minutes per week (with a range of 20–225 minutes). Individual sessions were as short as ten minutes in some institutions, while one school gave 75 minutes to each of its three periods.

However, a more consistent pattern emerges when examining the role of senior managers. In well over 80 per cent of cases one specific person has overall responsibility for pastoral care – most often a deputy head teacher. At the same time, those schools where all members of the senior management team (SMT) have some pastoral responsibility numbered fewer than one-third.

The sheer volume of responsibility allowance points given over to pastoral care in some schools raises serious questions about the efficient and effective management of resources. If one accepts what I have suggested regarding the existence of a lack of shared understanding, coherence and whole school planning, then one is forced to the conclusion that, in many schools, large numbers of personnel and significant financial resources are being poured into an area whose purpose is at best unclear, and has little direct relationship with the organization's primary learning objective.

Such concerns are intensified when one considers that the teaching time given over to pastoral delivery is, in the majority of cases, equivalent to that in some academic subjects, and in certain schools is on a par with provision for full GCSE courses. In addition, instances of very short time periods once more raise fears that pastoral time is merely, for some, an extension of registration for administrative purposes. Certainly, it is unlikely that any meaningful dialogue or learning experience can take place under such conditions.

One need only look at many secondary SMTs to find evidence of the ongoing division between the pastoral and academic domains. The notion of the 'pastoral supremo', with a pastoral background, line managing heads of year, via systems and structures separated from issues of curriculum management, is still familiar regardless of some movement in recent years. At the same time, other members of SMT often continue to have no oversight or responsibility whatsoever for issues within the pastoral domain. When one considers that SMTs are the breeding ground for almost all our secondary headteachers, it is perhaps unsurprising that dismantling such barriers in favour of a whole school approach is not necessarily easy.

Towards more effective management arrangements for the support of learning

Accepting that any attempt to succeed in providing an effective entitlement to pastoral care and PSE must begin with schools asking fundamental questions as to their purposes and priorities, uncertainties remain as to the most appropriate structure and systems for their delivery. I do not suggest that any one model can deliver the answer; schools will need to adopt measures most suited to their specific stage of organizational development. As a headteacher, I inherited (in my current school) a model of pastoral provision demonstrating many of the classic traits of Bell and Maher's (1986) early phases of development, alongside evidence of significant academic underperformance. In our determination to raise the achievement and attainment of students, we have embarked upon a change programme designed to address these issues. A number of steps have already been undertaken, with others to come. From this experience has developed a broad policy for the reform of pastoral management, the key points of which are as follows:

- The notion that a secondary school requires a single person to have overall and discrete responsibility for pastoral care should be discontinued. In its place there should be an insistence that all members of SMT have specific pastoral line management responsibilities, a situation easily achievable by, for example, attaching each senior manager to a specific year group or house. Such changes have the potential to extend the personal and professional development of staff, broadening their knowledge regarding all aspects of teaching and learning. There are clear benefits to whole school management from the knowledge brought back into SMT by members now in a position to make a more balanced and comprehensive contribution to debate. At the same time, the system has the capacity to develop and reinforce greater shared understanding of the purposes of pastoral provision.

    While the precise line management relationship between senior and middle managers will need to be clarified within individual institutions, it should be founded on supporting pastoral teams in ensuring quality provision. Focusing on issues agreed as priorities within SMT ensures consistency in the agendas addressed by pastoral teams. In addition, this allows schools to concentrate on developing systems for monitoring the quality of pastoral provision, including the design of appropriate metrics for evaluation of performance and the setting of targets linked to improvements in learning. There is no reason why pastoral managers should be any less subject to the processes of accountability than heads of curriculum areas; accepting responsibility for gathering and analysing both quantitative and qualitative data and devising strategies for improvement.

    These measures have the potential to assist in breaking down the pastoral/academic divide in schools, not least in sending out clear messages to all members of the school community regarding the contribution effective pastoral care can make to raising achievement. It is interesting to note that the increasing move towards having only one deputy headteacher within small to medium secondary schools is already forcing serious reconsideration of senior management roles and responsibilities.

- Traditional posts of responsibility such as head of year, head of lower school, should be replaced by key stage curriculum co-ordinators or year curriculum co-ordinators. In my school we have now settled on the title 'Achievement Co-ordinator' as most appropriate for our particular circumstances. Use of the term 'curriculum' emphasizes the school's primary function, with the notion of co-ordination suggesting the need for someone to be responsible for an overview of the whole curriculum experience on offer to a particular group of pupils, information on their individual progress, and proposals for action to bring about improvement. At the same time it sends out clear messages to all staff as to what this manager should be concentrating her/his efforts on. This job specification will radically alter the qualities, knowledge and skills required to manage in this area, with a clear shift away from a counsellor providing emotional or disciplinary support, to someone with a wide knowledge of teaching and learning strategies (including the processes involved in pupil learning) and the ability to advise and support subject areas.

  Opportunities for further professional development should be significantly enhanced; with teachers acquiring the skills and experiences to move into a broad range of senior management posts, rather than being set firmly on the 'pastoral' or 'academic' route at what may be an early stage in their career.

- 'The role of form tutors in the academic development of their tutees has frequently been peripheral – even incidental – rather than central.' Shaw's (1994) comments only serve to emphasize our continued failure to ensure that support for learning and achievement is at the heart of the provision of pastoral care. We need to concentrate our time on a dialogue about teaching and learning, as opposed to coverage of 'topics' which we have difficulty in delivering elsewhere.

  In order to perform effectively in this role, teachers require greater knowledge and understanding of learning processes. As outlined in Section One, this includes such areas as structured target-setting, monitoring and review skills, developing a shared vocabulary for talking to students about learning and interpreting information from a wide range of subject areas. Such a development will not happen overnight; it requires a commitment to in-service training and support which must be ongoing.

- Teachers responsible for, and actively teaching in, curriculum areas need to re-examine certain aspects of their work in the light of the changes suggested above. In those schools where the pastoral system has been viewed primarily as providing disciplinary support, departments will need to review their own strategies for managing behaviour; in particular regarding the impact of the student's curriculum experiences on their attentiveness and receptiveness, and how appropriate the learning task is for individual pupils.

  At the same time departments should examine schemes of work closely in an attempt to provide opportunities for subject teachers to undertake specialist tutoring with individuals or small groups. Where learning is organized in such a way as to allow for ongoing monitoring, review and target setting, not only does this raise achievement in the subject, but it also provides the pastoral tutor with feedback of an increasingly high quality.

- Schools should look closely at the structure of, and agendas for, their formal calendered meetings. For example, year teams need to focus much more closely on issues of teaching and learning. However, more importantly, institutions should ask themselves whether maintaining a pattern of professional dialogue organized predominantly around either the 'pastoral' or 'curriculum' domain, is the most appropriate way of supporting the school's primary objectives. Increasing the opportunities for teachers to meet in small cross-curricular groups to share ideas about teaching and learning, enhances dissemination of good practice and thereby promotes increases in student achievement.

- Where a school succeeds in creating the conditions under which effective tutoring can take place, pastoral tutors quickly begin to build up a very detailed overall picture of the performance of individual students, including patterns which may be emerging regarding particular strengths and weaknesses. A significant opportunity is therefore created to re-examine the most effective arrangements for consultation with parents.

    The traditional pattern of subject based consultation on a specific evening at a given time provokes criticism from both parents and teachers. Many parents may experience genuine difficulties in attending due to a range of factors, e.g. work patterns or childcare, especially where they are required to be available for perhaps two or three hours, much of which time is spent waiting to meet teachers. At the same time, teachers complain that the inability or unwillingness of some parents to attend means that they fail to make contact in cases, often, where the need is the greatest.

    An increasing number of secondary schools, including my own, have now moved to a system of 'Home/School Review Meetings'. Consultation regarding a student's performance across all subjects is led by the form tutor, with a week being set aside for appointments. Parents come into school for approximately twenty minutes, at a time which is convenient to them (or in some cases teachers go out to the home), to meet with an individual with whom they have already established a relationship. Dialogue can concentrate on celebrating areas of achievement across the curriculum and targeting areas for improvement. Parents leave with a clear picture of what their children need to do in order to raise their performance.

    Such a system can, in my experience, have a dramatic impact on the level of parental involvement; more so in those areas where adults may not feel comfortable coming into school, in particular to be part of a large formal event. Certainly, the response of the OFSTED Inspection Team reporting on my own organization, to the major increase in levels of parental involvement brought about by such changes was very

positive – leaving no doubt as to their judgement that the strengthen-
ing of the partnership between home and school would result in a
raising of achievement.

Implementing change: some considerations

Attempts to implement change will meet varied levels of resistance
according to the specific circumstances of each school. However, in some
instances this resistance will be formidable; the 'pastoral lobby', deeply
embedded in hierarchical management structures, feeling threatened,
devalued and de-skilled. Such parochial self-interest is absolutely understandable, many caring teachers having invested a significant proportion
of their careers in supporting existing pastoral care arrangements, which
in return have given them status and self-esteem. Whatever one's stage
of organizational development, planning the way forward will require
careful consideration.

There have been countless attempts throughout the past twenty years
– in both the private and public sectors – to identify the reasons why some
organizations manage change successfully and others do not. Aitken and
Saunders (1995), describing a recent research project in 63 companies,
highlight, among other things, the importance of: demonstrating commitment from the outset through the behaviour of the top team; maintaining
a clear sense of direction, focus and pace; identifying all stakeholders,
investing time in gaining and sustaining their involvement, and valuing
their contribution.

Certainly, the adoption of such strategies is consistent with the
position outlined at the beginning of this chapter, regarding the necessity
of a whole school approach to curriculum planning. However, as Beer *et
al.* (1990) concluded, there has been a long-held belief among change
management theorists that changes in attitudes result in changes in
behaviour. According to this model, change is like a conversion experience; 'once people have got religion, changes in their behaviour will surely
follow'. They suggest that this notion is fundamentally flawed, and that,
in fact, the change process works in exactly the opposite direction. They
insist that individual behaviour is powerfully shaped by the organizational roles that people play and, therefore, the most effective way to
change behaviour is to put people into a new organizational context
which imposes new roles, responsibilities and relationships on them. This
creates a situation that, in a sense, forces new attitudes and behaviour on
people.

On the basis of my own observations and experience within individual
schools and across LEAs, I believe that such a perspective has much to
commend it. This is not to say that time spent in developing a shared
sense of vision and purpose is not important; on the contrary, it plays a
valuable role in supporting an integrated change effort. However, it will
not, in itself, spread change rapidly through the entire organization.

As Beer observes, once an organization has defined new roles and
responsibilities, people need to develop the competencies to make the new
set-up work. The very existence of teams with new goals and account-
abilities will force learning. Changes in roles, responsibilities and
relationships foster new skills and attitudes. At the same time, changed

patterns of co-ordination will also increase participation, collaboration and information sharing among staff.

Changes embarked on in one of my former schools provide a good illustration of such a process in action. Following the retirement of a long-serving 'pastoral deputy', senior management persuaded the governors that it was no longer necessary for one person to have discrete responsibility for pastoral matters, and such a position was made clear in the ensuing recruitment literature. The initial response to such a move among heads of year was panic and confusion; for many years they had dealt with one specific person to whom they passed on problems and who was usually available to react to their needs. Such a situation was now to be replaced with a line management system linking each year head to a different senior manager. While in some instances these managers had no particular pastoral 'expertise', in all cases they would not be permanently 'on call' to deal with referrals.

Within weeks of the following term, significant changes were evident in the attitudes and behaviour of heads of year. Removal of the 'safety net' which the existence of the pastoral deputy had provided, meant that increasingly pastoral managers began to make their own decisions as to the appropriate action to take, with a subsequent fall in the number of referrals to senior management. At the same time, year heads welcomed the opportunity which line management meetings brought to discuss ideas for future developments, and such a proactive approach began to be reflected in the nature of discussions within pastoral teams. Moreover, pastoral managers became increasingly unwilling to accept being used as a repository for disciplinary problems, especially where departments were not following agreed procedures, forcing curriculum areas to re-examine their own practice. Perhaps the most telling comment came from the head of year (with over three decades of experience in a pastoral role) who informed me (her line manager) at the end of the first term that, while she had never felt so supported during her career, for the first time she felt she was really being allowed to manage.

If the change process is to be implemented successfully, management must provide the right support. However, by ascribing new roles and responsibilities to staff, as in the case above, an interesting development follows. Teachers come to see what kind of new skills they need and ask for formal training to develop these further. Since these courses grow directly out of their own experiences, they tend to be far more focused and useful than traditional training programmes.

CONCLUDING THOUGHTS

Despite claims from many teachers that recent legislation has severely limited their professional autonomy with regard to curriculum planning, there is evidence that some schools are continuing to demonstrate the ability to interpret such rules in a way that allows them to maintain a sense of coherence, and deliver quality pastoral provision which supports learning. However, such a position is by no means universal. There remains, in a number of schools, a lack of coherence and consensus regarding the nature of pastoral provision, with too much emphasis continuing to be placed on a body of knowledge to be covered, as opposed to the development of processes designed to improve students' learning potential. In addition, a significant proportion of pastoral managers remain wedded to a reactive model of pastoral care which highlights notions of 'welfare' and support for 'non-academic' aspects of schooling. Within such organizations, even where considerable time is given to delivery of the pastoral curriculum, the tutoring process is often insufficiently focused on developing the skills and abilities students need in order to take greater responsibility for their work – thereby enabling them to become more effective learners. At the same time, opportunities are forgone to learn about our own practice and how it could be improved, in particular with regard to enhancing the levels of attentiveness, receptiveness and appropriateness in our classrooms.

In accepting the fact that there is a sound legal justification for a continuing pastoral dimension in the secondary curriculum, we have to address some fundamental questions regarding precisely how pastoral programmes can contribute towards meeting our aims. For many organizations, this will require a significant reappraisal of existing systems and structures for delivering pastoral care. Any such determination to ensure increased support for learning will raise serious questions regarding the qualities required to become an effective pastoral manager. Furthermore, it will present a real challenge to what are often long-established management arrangements; we should be under no illusion as to the resistance this is likely to encounter in some secondary schools.

It is surprising that pastoral care has not been subjected to much closer scrutiny, in the political upheaval which education has witnessed in recent years. This is not to say it has avoided criticism from either end of the political spectrum; the right seeing it as 'do-gooding' which stresses welfare at the expense of achievement, while certain left-wing critics remain convinced that pastoral care is primarily concerned with socializing deviants and maintaining a system of 'control'. In my view, there is some truth in both observations. Moreover, when one considers the sheer level of personnel, time and materials committed to pastoral provision in the secondary sector, it is likely that some very serious questions will be asked in the near future, regarding the efficient employment of resources in this area. If we are to avoid being subjected once more to the ignominy of ill thought-out and externally imposed change, the answer is in our own hands: to ensure we are very clear about what we mean by pastoral care and precisely how it will improve learning in our schools.

NOTE

1. *The National Curriculum and Its Assessment: Final Report* (January 1994) produced by SCAA Chair, Sir Ron Dearing. This included a series of proposals adopted, for a new curriculum model for age 5–16.

REFERENCES

Aitken, A. and Saunders, I. (1995) Vision only works if communicated. *People Management*, Dec.

Aristotle, *The Politics (Book 8)*. Loeb Classical Library.

Beer, M., Eisenstat, R. A. and Spector, B. (1990) Why change programmes don't produce change. *Harvard Business Review*, Dec.

Bell, L. and Maher, P. (1986) *Leading a Pastoral Team*. Oxford: Blackwell.

Bennett, R. (1996) *Corporate Strategy and Business Planning*. London: Pitman.

Best, R., Jarvis, C. and Ribbins, P. (eds) (1980) *Perspectives on Pastoral Care*. London: Heinemann.

Best, R., Jarvis, C. and Ribbins, P. (1997) Pastoral care: concept and process. *British Journal of Educational Studies*, **25**(2), 124–35.

Best, R., Lang, P., Lodge, C. and Watkins, C. (eds) (1995) *Pastoral Care and Personal-Social Education: Entitlement and Provision*. London: Cassell.

Best, R., Ribbins, P., Jarvis, C. and Oddy, D. (1983). *Education and Care*. London: Heinemann.

Betterton, H. and Nash, J. (1996) *Academic Tutoring*. Sutton LEA.

Blyth, W. A. L. (1988) *Learning Is More Important than Teaching*. Leicester: University of Leicester.

Buckley, J. (1980) The care of learning – some implications for school organisation. In Best, R. *et al.* (eds) *Perspectives on Pastoral Care*. London: Heinemann.

Calvert, M. and Henderson, J. (1995) Leading the team: managing pastoral care in a secondary setting. In Bell, J. and Harrison, B. T. (eds) *Vision and Values in Managing Education*. London: Fulton.

Department of Education and Science (1989) *Report of Her Majesty's Inspectors on Pastoral Care in Secondary Schools: An Inspection of Some Aspects of Pastoral Care in 1987–8*. London: DES.

Duncan, C. (1988). *Pastoral Care: An Anti-Racist / Multi-Cultural Perspective*. Oxford: Blackwell.

Education Reform Act (1988) London: HMSO.

Gothard, W. P. and Goodhew, E. (1987) *Guidance and the Changing Curriculum*. London: Croom Helm.

Griffiths, P. (1995) Guidance and tutoring. In Best, R. *et al.* (eds) *Pastoral Care and Personal-Social Education*. London: Cassell.

Hamblin, D. (ed.) (1981) *The Problems and Practice of Pastoral Care*. Oxford: Blackwell.

Hargreaves, D. H. and Hopkins, D. (eds) (1994) *Development Planning for School Improvement*. London: Cassell.

Hopkins, D., Ainscow, M. and West, M. (1994) *School Improvement in an Era of Change*. London: Cassell.

Kyriacou, C. (1986) *Effective Teaching in Schools*. Simon and Schuster.

Lodge, C. (1995) School management for pastoral care and PSE. In Best, R. *et al.* (eds) *Pastoral Care and Personal-Social Education*. London: Cassell.

Lofthouse, M. (1994) Managing learning. In Bush, T. and West-Burnham, J. (eds) *The Principles of Educational Management*. Harlow: Longman.

McGuiness, J. (1989) *A Whole-School Approach to Pastoral Care*. London: Kogan Page.

Marland, M. (1980) The pastoral curriculum. In Best, R. *et al.* (eds) *Perspectives on Pastoral Care*. London: Heinemann.

Marland, M. (1989) *The Tutor and the Tutor Group*. Harlow: Longman.

Marland, M. (1995) The whole curriculum. In Best, R. *et al.* (eds) *Pastoral Care and Personal-Social Education*. London: Cassell.

Munby, S. (1995) Assessment and pastoral care : sense, sensitivity and standards. In Best, R. *et al.* (eds) *Pastoral Care and Personal-Social Education*. London: Cassell.

OFSTED (1995) *Guidance on the Inspection of Secondary Schools*. London: HMSO.

Power, S. (1996) *The Pastoral and the Academic: Conflict and Contradiction in the Curriculum*. London: Cassell.

Raymond, J. (1985) *Implementing Pastoral Care in Schools*. London: Croom Helm.

Ribbins, P. M. (1985) Editorial: three reasons for thinking more about schooling and welfare. In Ribbins, P. (ed.) *Schooling and Welfare*. London: Falmer Press.

Shaw, M. (1994) Current issues in pastoral management. *Pastoral Care in Education*, **12**(4), 37–41.

Waterhouse, P. (1991) *Tutoring*. Stafford: Network Educational Press.

Watkins, C. (1995) Personal-social education and the whole curriculum. In Best, R. *et al.* (eds) *Pastoral Care and Personal-Social Education*. London: Cassell.

White, M. (1991) *Self-Esteem*. London: Daniels.

Williamson, D. (1980) Pastoral care or pastoralization. In Best, R. *et al.* (eds) *Perspectives on Pastoral Care*. London: Heinemann.

CHAPTER 3

Fitness for purpose: self-care and the pastoral tutor
Carol Hall

INTRODUCTION

This chapter focuses on the challenge to pastoral care teams to promote and develop their own self-care strategies alongside pupil support stratlossegies. A central leadership responsibility is to frame the understanding of the importance of tutor self-care within an institutional context and create systems which enable tutors to monitor their own developmental needs. A key role for the tutor within a 'health' focused pastoral system is to encourage and promote pro-social attitudes and behaviours in all members of the learning community. The emphasis on health begins with pastoral tutors and argues that teachers prioritizing their own social, emotional, physical and spiritual well-being have all but disappeared from the educational agenda. If we are serious in our intention to support and guide pupils to lead fulfilling and worthwhile lives, then it is vital to ensure that we remain fit for that purpose. The notion of the fully-functioning individual is discussed and how teachers might sustain their self-esteem even under stress is demonstrated. Management strategies for promoting and maintaining teacher effectiveness in the pastoral role are proposed. Supervision, peer support groups and mentoring as school-based support systems are outlined. The continuing failure to address the personal growth and development of the pastoral care tutor in schools, despite the growing evidence of research which outlines the relationship between teacher effectiveness and psychological health, is a management issue which we ignore at our pupils' cost.

THE ANSWER WAS STARING ME IN THE FACE . . .

In this chapter I want us to take one step back, out of the turbulence of the school and its insistent demands, to a quieter, calmer, more reflective space. For a brief time, as the image of the school gate recedes, I want to tell you about a concern that has been growing in me for the last ten years. During that time, I have worked in the field of human relations with people from the so-called caring professions. Their work is people-focused and concerned to offer care and support within a professional framework. They are predominantly drawn from education but also from nursing, social services, the ministry, probation, the police and counselling. The human relations courses include: interpersonal skills training, counselling skills, group dynamics and self-negotiated learning (Hall and Hall, 1988). This work is influenced to a large extent by the work of humanistic psychologists such as Maslow (1954), Rogers (1980) and Egan (1994), all of whom place great emphasis on the basic human drive for self-actualization or the realization of our full capacity to live and learn. The work is experiential and involves participants in a degree of self-reflection in relation to their own history of social and emotional learning. Inevitably, this is at times an uncomfortable process but one which may reveal deep insight into the self and others (Bowes, 1988). A basic assumption underpinning this work is that the teacher's own quality of life can have a direct impact upon the professional capacity to care and support the development of pupils for good or ill (Mahoney, 1991).

Out of this work grew an intuition, a hunch, a sneaking suspicion which has now evolved into a conviction. My conviction is that teachers are very tuned in to the needs and concerns of their pupils and see this as a moral, as well as a professional, responsibility. However, even though they may be alert to the needs of others, they may be less good at attending to their own emotional growth. Let me give you an example of a pastoral situation where a tutor may be deskilled from most effectively supporting a pupil. A grief-stricken child will need the tender support of an understanding, empathic tutor. However, if that tutor has unresolved emotional questions about coping with death, loss or grief in his or her own life, then effective support may be compromised. Common forms of emotional defensiveness might include unwillingness or fear of letting the child express feelings connected with the pain of the loss – particularly crying or sobbing in public or even in private with the tutor. A desire by the teacher to pretend that nothing is amiss and behave as though nothing has happened: rationalizing this as talking about it only makes it worse. A secret impatience with the child if the loss affects school work or behaviour for any prolonged period. A wish to hurry them up to 'get over it' and try to return to 'normal'. In a vivid example such as this, it is possible to see that emotional avoidance connected with a specific life experience of the tutor can be touched off by direct connection with a pupil in need, rendering the pastoral support needed at such a time inadequate for the healing process.

Pastoral leaders are often both creative and thoughtful in the ways they develop school-wide systems which support pastoral care initiatives (Best *et al.*, 1995), as other chapters of this book testify, but are frankly not very good at taking care of themselves emotionally or knowing how to develop helping and supporting systems for their teams in schools. This will have a knock-on effect on their ability to operationalize, in human relations terms, the desired outcomes of pastoral systems. Without the quality of the direct person-to-person contact any pastoral systems are meaningless.

Recently, I had the opportunity to work with a group of headteachers. The theme of the day was effective school management and human relations. In emphasizing the relationship between teacher effectiveness and the individual's capacity to be self-nurturing and self-directing, I was pressing home the message of the importance of taking care of yourself, not only intellectually, but also physically, emotionally and spiritually. Afterwards, the group began talking about the impact of the session. One of them said tearfully that in all her years as a teacher with management responsibilities, it was the first time anyone had told her that she had a professional responsibility to take care of herself or stressed the importance of this in relation to maintaining her own capacity to care for the well-being of others. The message which over the years she had so powerfully internalized was that her primary duty and responsibility were to care and support the welfare of her pupils, secondly her staff and thirdly the wider school community. She did not figure in the list of individuals or groups who needed attention. Her sense of meaning and purpose in her vocation was to educate, guide and nurture the development of others. She had never allowed the possibility that she herself might need personal support or social and emotional guidance in a professional setting. Or that she might have to make the space in her own life to make her own growth a priority.

Try answering these few simple questions honestly. How many times in the last month have you:

- spent a weekend at home when you haven't worried about work?
- taken a long walk in the countryside just to enjoy nature?
- confided in someone you trust about difficulties you face?
- laughed until you cried?
- cried – and not just at a sentimental film?
- read great literature, really listened to music, visited an art gallery or museum, looked at a great building?
- felt loved?
- done something for the sheer fun or joy of it?
- told someone you loved them and really meant it?
- really struggled to improve a difficult relationship?
- been overcome by the beauty of a moment?
- danced or exercised until you could feel your own heart beat?
- done something creative: painted a picture, written a poem, worked in the garden, built something with your own hands, played an instrument or sang a song?
- slept like a baby and woke up feeling refreshed?
- left your briefcase at work – intentionally?
- talked to someone about your hopes and fears – about things which really mean a lot to you?
- stood up for a principle you really cared about?
- counted your blessings?

The experience of talking to and working with hundreds of teachers at all levels of the organizational hierarchy confirmed my hunch that there was a tendency to give personal development issues a low priority. This was characterized variously as selfish, not what we are paid for, the kids' needs are more important than mine or just a general feeling that the culture of the school was opposed to the very idea of addressing teachers' social or emotional needs. It was not a subject that could find a legitimate outlet for expression *even among pastoral leaders or their teams*. This to me was very surprising as so much has been talked and written about within the educational world in relation to the professional development of teachers (Hargreaves and Fullan, 1992), it seemed impossible that this could be the case. Hadn't teachers had training opportunities, signed up for higher education courses, done research degrees, gathered together to pool knowledge, information and resources in families of schools and used initiatives such as TVEI to develop classroom practice?

Nevertheless, there was still a large and important part of the jigsaw missing and this to me was at the very heart of the picture. What had been missing were the opportunities and spaces to focus on the *person of the teacher*, understanding that this was a legitimate and necessary condition for sustaining teacher effectiveness, not a pointless navel-gazing exercise. To explore not just the intellectual, cognitive processes in becoming an effective pastoral tutor, but to have the reflective space to explore the emotional component of that development. To share how it really feels to be a teacher today and how focusing on the development of self-awareness and self-esteem can promote increased feelings of greater self-control and lessen stress (Abaci *et al.*, 1997). Such a commitment to personal growth is not a self-indulgence which stops us getting on with our real jobs but a necessity to sustain us to do our jobs more efficiently and effectively.

The professional development model, while enormously important, can actually widen the gap between teachers' sense of who they are right now and what they should be as perfect professionals. The gap between the rhetoric of professional development and the individual's capacity to live out these ideals on a day-to-day basis can only be bridged by a profound acknowledgement that teachers, particularly and most vividly in their role as pastoral carers, need to develop their capacity to both think and feel, to develop what Goleman (1995) calls their 'emotional intelligence'. The debates around professional development are largely posited on the assumption that teachers are in a state of psychological and emotional readiness or willingness to take up their responsibility for professional development. What was apparent to me was that firstly many teachers are not emotionally in a position to devote any energy to their develop-ment and also that reading all the books in the world may not change one iota how they feel about their own capacity to develop. In the end, it is so much whistling in the wind. Teachers need to be given permission (and as importantly give themselves permission) to put their own social and emotional self at the top of the agenda and this needs to be legitimated by school policy and strategically implemented by the provision of teacher support systems. These will be discussed later in this chapter.

THE IMPORTANCE OF SELF-CARE FOR TEACHERS IN THE PASTORAL ROLE

McGuiness (1989) makes a compelling case when he argues that there is 'no opting out' of the pastoral dimension in the role of teacher. As a profession, we broadly acknowledge that the provision of specialist pastoral teams is not an invitation to leave it to the experts, but a whole school recognition that the real cost of effective pastoral care needs to be costed in terms of time, training and leadership. The pastoral dimension of the teaching role is enacted on a day-to-day basis through the delivery of the curriculum, as well as in the more subtle but pervasive sense of the quality of the interpersonal relationships between teachers and students. The quality of these relationships is inextricably linked, both positively and negatively, to the learning outcomes in the classrooms. 'No opting out', though, places a considerable emotional as well as professional obligation on teachers to 'care'. In fact we demand that there is a duty to care. Kottler and Kottler (1993) list the duties of care, the interpersonal dimension of a teacher's work, in the following way. Remember that each of these items may occur singly or in combination in any one school day or even hour!

- Respond to children's emotional needs
- Resolve interpersonal conflicts
- Conduct parent conferences
- Identify children suffering from abuse, neglect, drug abuse and a variety of emotional problems and make appropriate referrals where necessary
- Assess children's development transitions, and guide their continued physical, emotional, social and spiritual growth, in addition to their cognitive development
- Participate in Individualized Learning Programmes
- Function as a problem-solver for those children in the throes of crisis.

Clearly, to be the kind of teacher who can respond both appropriately and consistently to these enormously important demands, takes not only emotional maturity but a degree of interpersonal stamina also. If we turn this list around and ask ourselves whether we are able to perform those functions of care for ourselves, then we begin to see just what it takes for pastoral tutors to develop their capacity to sustain nurturing relationships with students. How would you respond to the following statements?

- I am in touch with my emotional needs and I can express my feelings congruently.
- I am able to resolve my own inner conflicts and be solution-orientated in my dealings with others.
- I am able to identify issues from my own past which may impinge on my ability to work with pupils undergoing similar stressors, for example dealing with bereavement or abuse and separating my own feelings from theirs.
- I am aware of my own imperfections and can truthfully assess my own development needs – emotional, physical, spiritual and social. I stay in touch with the core values that drive my life and integrity.
- I am proactive in planning for my own personal growth because this is my responsibility.

- I know how to ask for help and support assertively when I feel in crisis. I can take help when offered.

Self-care is not merely a function of maintaining intra- and interpersonal functioning but a willingness to commit to staying fit and healthy physically. This has the additional spin-off of ensuring entitlement of pastoral provision throughout the week. Most of us will have experienced the Friday afternoon syndrome – pupils are fractious, itching to get away for a weekend break, teachers are exhausted and ready for the final bell. Inevitably, this is the time when incidents which require tutor attention are likely to occur. A physically and emotionally exhausted tutor will not have the reserves of energy to deal patiently and sensitively with pupils in crisis.

Rogers and Freiberg (1994, p. 259) usefully summarize Aspey and Roebuck's research on the relationship between interpersonal functioning and levels of physical fitness. Among Aspey and Roebuck's (1976) conclusions were that:

Fatigue, poor nutrition, and lack of physical exercise are deterrents to positive interpersonal relationships. The data from subsequent work suggest strongly that physical fitness is necessary for sustaining constructive interpersonal relationships across long periods of time. It seems that all teachers who understand constructive human relationships can be humane for short periods of time, but their levels of physical fitness determine the durability of their interpersonal facilitation.

What is evident from the research is that no matter how good you are in the pastoral role, if you do not have the physical stamina to stay focused, patient and alert, then relatively small incidents may blow up out of all proportion. Aspey and Roebuck also show that physically fit teachers were scoring higher on Friday afternoons for teacher responsiveness towards students, while the general pattern is for teacher responsiveness to decline. Use the following checklist to evaluate your own commitment to staying healthy. How could you develop your own fitness or stamina?

Ask yourself the following questions: How committed am I to staying healthy? How many of the following statements honestly describe my current practice?

- I maintain a regular programme of aerobic exercise (30 minutes at least three times a week).
- I ensure that I eat a high proportion of fruit and vegetables in my diet.
- I only drink tea/coffee/alcohol in moderation.
- My weight remains constant and is about right for my age, height and gender.
- Where possible, I avoid foods which are high in salt, sugar, chemicals, fats or are highly refined.
- I avoid bingeing or crash diets.
- I drink plenty of water.

- I don't smoke.
- I take responsibility for staying healthy.
- I regularly create spaces for relaxation or meditation.
- I don't eat meals 'on the run'.
- I ensure that I get an adequate amount of sleep each night.

Maintaining a consistently good level of physical fitness overall can also serve a dual purpose of immunizing the individual against the debilitating effects of high levels of professional and personal stress (Kabat-Zinn, 1996).

BETWEEN A ROCK AND A HARD PLACE

McGuiness's (1989) stern reminder that there can be no opting out from pastoral responsibility also forces pastoral leaders to recognize that such a commitment, however worthy, does not come without its shadow side. The extent of the emotional toll that the interpersonal, pastoral dimension of the teacher's role exacts from day-to-day and week-to-week can be debilitating physically, emotionally and psychologically. This can result in *caring overload*. This process represents a burn-out of the individual's capacity to feel and respond to the needs of others. This is more likely to occur in those people who have failed to recognize the signs and symptoms of their own reduced capacity to respond humanely and failed to take appropriate self-care action.

One teacher I spoke to described the process like this:

Some days I feel like I am literally in the trenches. I drive to work, stuck in the usual queue of traffic and listen to politicians on the radio talking about falling standards and arguing about the best way to sack poor teachers. I arrive at school thinking about how I am going to survive the OFSTED inspection and then find all the car parking spaces are gone. Walking through the playground, I have to stop a major fight from breaking out and as I rush for cover in the staff room, my heart sinks because I can see there is the substitution list on the notice board. I know my name will be on it because there is always someone off sick. I find a letter in my pigeon-hole from a parent who says her son is being bullied and blames me for not stopping it. A colleague grabs me as I try to make a cup of coffee and bends my ear about his head of department, who is giving him a hard time. In the pre-school briefing, the head reminds us – as if we needed it – of the deadline for the end of term reports and, to cap it all, I know that the first lesson of the day is with a group of bored 15-year-olds who can't wait to get out of school. And all this before 9.00am! On days like this, it is difficult to get the energy to drag myself out of bed. When is anyone going to listen to me and how bad it can get sometimes? We are supposed to be there for the kids the whole time. When is anyone ever there for me?

Ask yourself the following questions:

- List the names of people you feel you can talk to in your life right now who are willing and able to listen carefully and non-judgementally – people who are on your side. When did you last have an important conversation about things that matter to you with these people? In the last week, month, year?

- When things aren't going your way, do you blame others, yourself, the system? Or do you focus on what you can control and work to improve those things? Can you stop worrying about things which you have no control over and take responsibility for your own behaviour?

- Do you understand what assertive behaviour is and recognize your own patterns of passive, manipulative and aggressive behaviours?

- Can you offer support to other colleagues who may be experiencing emotional difficulties and listen empathically and non-judgementally? Are you someone whom others feel they can trust and confide in about things that really matter – and not just complain or gossip?

Teachers may acknowledge the necessity of the pastoral dimension of their role at a rational level and pay lip-service to the idea 'we're all tutors of pastoral care' but emotionally shy away from what such a commitment inevitably means. Many heads of year will recognize the reluctance of colleagues to take part in relationship education, denying any 'expertise' in that area! This retreat is understandable when there is so obvious a neglect in relation to the professional entitlement for the development of emotional intelligence in teachers (Goleman, 1996). Little emphasis is placed on assessing the level of emotional intelligence or capability for development in would-be teachers at the teacher training stage and there is a dearth of development opportunities for interpersonal, personal and counselling skills development in in-service provision. This is coupled with the absence of supervision and emotional support opportunities within the school for members of pastoral teams.

Too little attention is given to the ways in which we nurture and sustain our own ability to care. Paradoxically, it is taken for granted that teachers will be entitled to the institutional support which is essential for continuing professional development. In-service training and appraisal are in-built systems for ensuring professional renewal at a cognitive level, but still leave teachers hungry for a place to talk legitimately about their feelings. What has been so signally missing from the equation is the importance of personal development and the appropriate mechanisms which support it. Teacher 'health' has been largely defined as a function of the academic or intellectual ability to fit the role. Important questions about the emotional maturity of teachers (Rogers and Freiberg, 1994) and their continuing fitness to care for our young people are left too often to chance or fate. We need to acknowledge as a profession that the ultimate price we pay personally for such neglect may be higher than we want to pay. Take a look at the table opposite. Mahoney (1991) adapts Kahill's model of the symptoms of burnout in the caring professions.

How many of these symptoms have you experienced in the last six months? Where would you look for help if you needed it? Would you know how to recognize and support a colleague who was displaying some of these symptoms in your pastoral team?

Table 3.1 Common symptoms of professional burnout

1. *Physical*
   Exhaustion or chronic fatigue
   Headaches
   Increased vulnerability to colds and flu
   Sleep disturbances
   Back pain
   Gastrointestinal problems

2. *Behavioural*
   Increased alcohol use
   Increased caffeine and nicotine consumption
   Increased drug use (licit and illicit)
   Increased absenteeism and social withdrawal
   Overeating

3. *Emotional and Psychological*
   Reduced sense of self-efficacy
   Negative attitudes about self, clients, work and life
   Increased irritability, anger and hostility
   Depression
   Anxiety
   Emotional distancing and depersonalization

THE 'FULLY-FUNCTIONING' TUTOR: SELF-AWARENESS AND SELF-ESTEEM

Carl Rogers (1963; Rogers and Freiberg, 1994) uses the term 'fully-functioning' to describe a person who remains open to experience and is able to live to the full in each moment of his or her life. This ability to stay in touch with the moment, 'the here and now', is the quality which serves as the bedrock of our ability to *empathize* with others and to see the world as others may see and experience it. Coupled with this is the ability to have a deep and abiding trust in one's own ability to grow and develop in constructive ways. This trust in the self is mirrored in the trust that we have in others – that they too have the potential to develop in healthy, constructive ways, given the appropriate conditions for growth. Offering *positive regard* to others is the outer expression of this organismal trust. Being fully alive to the 'feeling self' connects us up and keeps us connected to these deep levels of inner wisdom. We are our own best experts. This *congruence*, the ability to be in touch with feelings and express them in ways which convey the depth of our felt experience, is the way that others recognize the genuineness, the realness of us as human beings; without front or facade. We dare to express our real self, because we trust that the real self is worthy of love and the regard of others. Congruence, positive regard and empathy are the core conditions which underpin mature human relationships (Rogers, 1962). To these core conditions Brian Thorne (1985) adds one other – tenderness. Schools, as we all know, can be brutal places at times. Interpersonal tenderness is essential if we are to permit our pupils to disclose their vulnerability to us in pastoral encounters. No child ever talked about their pain when being ordered, bullied or harassed by a teacher short of time and anxious to get to the next lesson.

O'Connell and O'Connell (1980) describe the four interlinked processes of personality integration as:

1. The continual development of one's *intellectual or cognitive* function.
2. The steady unfolding and enrichment of one's *emotional* repertory.
3. The determination to direct one's own destiny.
4. The quest to relate oneself to one's world.

This is the work of the self-in-process. It is not about being the perfect person but a fundamental understanding that learning is a life-long process which is mediated through our own awareness. This faculty of self-awareness needs to be constantly and self-consciously attended to, if the vicissitudes of everyday life are not to erode its edge.

In short, the fully-functioning person has an enduring self-esteem and can maintain the sense of being a worthwhile person, even when the going gets tough – and it will. This ability is born out of the experience of childhood. Generally speaking, individuals with high self-esteem are lucky enough to receive consistently positive esteem messages from people who love them when they are growing up and also receive positive reinforcement for assertive or self-directed behaviours. As adults, though, it is not enough to rely on the love and care of others to make us feel good about ourselves. We need to be alert to our own feelings and beliefs about our abilities and be prepared to struggle to raise our self-evaluation. We can do this through a dynamic process of learning about the self through the conscious development of our self-awareness.

It is a common misconception that just by 'feeling' or 'expressing feelings', we can learn about them. This is of course the first step – to be in touch with and express feelings – but it is only the first step. Learning about ourselves does not necessarily arise out of the experience of feelings or emotion. Think about the last time you felt really angry about something or someone. The experience of that emotion does not help you learn about what makes you angry or how to express it more con-structively next time, or even decide if it was the right person to be angry with. What helps you to engage in learning from the experience of anger is self-awareness. It is what Jon Kabatt-Zinn describes as the cave behind the waterfall (1996). The waterfall is our conscious mind, alive with thoughts, feelings, anxieties, worries, fears, hopes: sometimes in full flood, sometimes calmer. Self-awareness is the ability to step back, out of the turbulence of the waterfall, and contemplate in a qualitatively different place what is going on in your life right now. It is the ability to almost simultaneously disengage from the emotion and focus on what can be learned about the self and others out of the experience of the emotion. The development of this psychological disengagement comes from many sources. For some it is religious practice, yoga or meditation, for others it is being privileged to be alongside wise people who can almost magically facilitate growth. For others, it will be a realization that there is a need to take greater control or responsibility for their own futures. Pastoral tutors who are seeking this kind of development may be actively encouraged to participate in human relations or counselling courses, choosing learning opportunities which focus attention on the development of self-awareness.

Taking care of the self does not mean putting yourself first. The former is self-esteem, the latter selfishness. This is an important and enduring distinction. Scott Peck (1993) recounts an interesting piece of research, undertaken during his time as a psychotherapist in the American army. Interested in what made high fliers tick, he brought together a dozen or so men and women who fitted the bill. They were very successful in their careers, liked and respected by colleagues and in stable, happy, partnered relationships with children who were doing well at school and socially well adjusted. In short, these people had everything going for them. What was the secret of their success? Out of the research emerged a key factor. When asked to name the top priority in their lives, they all came up with the same answer – MYSELF. This is a vivid illustration that a positive self-esteem, what Peck calls 'self-love', leads not to selfishness and alienation in relationships, but to the capacity to understand that a loving accepting relationship with the self is the bedrock of the capacity to love and care for others. They were able to love and care because they felt loving and caring, not out of guilt or resentment or the expectations of others. Ask yourself the questions: What are my priorities in my life right now? Do I need to rethink this order?

The Californian Task Force was set up by the state legislature to investigate self-esteem and its relationship to the educational process. Dismayed at the continuing breakdown of social cohesion and its effects on young people (evident through drug abuse, teenage pregnancies, school drop-out and so on), the state legislature funded a large-scale study into self-esteem. The report was published in 1990. The Chair of the Task Force, Andrew Mecca, commented significantly that 'self-esteem is not some new-age, feel good approach. Rather it is part and parcel of personal and social responsibility.'

Reasoner and Dusa (1991), researchers on the task force, isolated five essential elements for the development of self-esteem. It is worth noting that these elements hold true for individual esteem and institutional esteem. They cite the following: a sense of security, self-awareness, the feeling of belonging, a sense of purpose and a sense of personal competence as the basis for maintaining a positive self-esteem. How, as pastoral leaders, do we actively seek to establish these conditions in our schools not just for our pupils but for ourselves? The recommendations of the report include the following: 'Self-esteem and responsibility must be woven into the total education programme' and 'Educate every educator through pre-service and in-service training in self-esteem and responsibility'.

Educating the educators must mean a willingness to explore personal levels of self-esteem and a willingness to work on those aspects of the self which need some attention through self-care.

GETTING THE SUPPORT YOU NEED: THE IMPORTANCE OF INSTITUTIONALLY-BASED CARE SYSTEMS: SUPERVISION, PEER SUPPORT AND MENTORING

Who will care and protect the carers?

(Juvenal, *Satire* vi, lines 347–8)

As a young, enthusiastic, newly-appointed head of Year 7 in a secondary school, I once had the opportunity to work with a young girl who had just made the difficult transfer from primary school. She was first brought to my attention by a French teacher, who complained that the girl was regularly late for lessons first thing in the morning, added to which she was not giving in her French homework on time. In class, the girl was not a behavioural problem, although her manner was distracted and she would often be found staring vacantly out of the window.

This did not seem to be a promising start to a career in secondary school and I began to unravel the story behind the girl's behaviour. I discovered a bleak picture. Her mother was earning her living through prostitution nightly in the family home. The father was not in contact with his children. There were six other siblings in the family and she was the eldest. Her mother was an alcoholic and suffered from epilepsy. The girl managed her mother's alcoholic episodes as well as her fits while taking responsibility for the younger siblings on a day-to-day basis. There was a palpable air of emotional vulnerability as well as a physical fragility about the girl. She was undernourished and looked bone-marrow weary. At 11 years of age it was obvious that she had seen more of 'life' than had many of her grown-up teachers.

I can recall vividly the feelings of despair I felt for her and her family as I became more acquainted with their desperation. The sense of uselessness that overcame me at times was overwhelming because I did not know what to do with feelings of anger, rage and despair both at the situation and at my insensitive colleague, to whom the most important priority was getting the French homework in on time.

I recount this story because the feelings I was left with were personally stressful for me and rendered me less effective in being clear about the goals and strategies which might make a difference. Some twenty years later, I understand that it was my own vulnerability that I took home with me. I felt sad, depressed and incompetent and it was my own need to make everything all right for people which interfered with taking positive assertive action. My self-esteem rested on the need to be seen by colleagues to be doing a good job 'managing' the situation. Part of that managing was proving to the French teacher that I was the sort of head of year who could effectively 'problem-solve' and persuade the girl of the necessity for learning French verbs in the disarray that was her life. Also, I needed to convince the pastoral deputy head that I had been the right choice in relation to the appointment. Owning up to my desperation didn't seem to be an option then.

Many of you reading this chapter will have similar instances to recount, when the emotional ripples of working with pupils' distress go far beyond the issue that was raised. Her distress spoke to all of us who were willing to hear it and posed questions for us as pastoral leaders which went beyond the desperation of her personal case. This was one child among many. I certainly would not want to claim that all pastoral work raises such potent images of family life nor would I want to say that schools should be focusing their energies on working with the so-called victims of social disadvantage. What I am concerned with is how to ensure tutor effectiveness in the pastoral role when faced with similarly heavy emotional demands on a daily basis. We first have to ensure our own psychological health and set up school processes which support this continuing health. Supervision for pastoral tutors and teams is one such process.

As Hawkins and Shohet (1992) remind us, members of the helping professions, teachers, social workers, doctors will often report feeling drained by giving support but receive very little support themselves. Coupled with this is their contention that helpers may in fact be addicted to helping, which is in essence a defence against receiving help themselves when they need it. The challenge institutionally is how to support pastoral tutors so that they can maintain their interpersonal competence to deal with the complexities of the human issues that are presented to them. Supervision is mandatory for counsellors (Bond, 1990) and routine for social workers and the practice is now growing in medical settings. As Hawkins and Shohet (1989) so succinctly put it: 'A good supervisory relationship is the best way we know to ensure that we stay open to ourselves and to our clients.'

They tell the illuminating story of miners in the 1920s who fought for what was called 'pit-head time'. This amounted to being given the right to time to wash off the dirt from the toil of the job, so that they could go home cleansed. Hawkins and Shohet point out that this is exactly the function that supervision is designed to fulfil.

Supervision is an institutionally-based process, which is intended to safeguard standards of professional practice through direct tutor support. In schools we might envision it as a relationship-led encounter between the pastoral tutor, who is encouraged to think of the form or year group as a caseload and bring issues which are currently 'hot' to discuss, and the supervisor, who will be a designated person, usually a pastoral team leader who has extended training in, and understanding of, counselling or counselling skills. Provision for supervisor training in this country is still quite patchy and can be expensive. The role of the supervisor ultimately is to ensure that the client, in this instance the pupil, is receiving the best possible support. The supervisory relationship does in fact share many similarities with the counselling relationship. It is confidential, has clearly defined time boundaries and works on social-emotional issues in order to make the individual more effective in everyday life. Personal issues for the tutor which arise out of the experience of the pastoral role can be worked on legitimately and coping strategies discussed.

Smith, in Palmer *et al.* (1996), points out two different and distinct areas of supervisory practice. He calls them supervisor-centred and supervisee-centred. Supervisor-centred is when the supervisor offers advice, suggests ways forward or approaches with the client, while the latter is focused on enabling the counsellor or tutor to make his or her own decisions about practice. The former is what might be termed managerial or educational supervision; the latter supportive supervision (Hawkins and Shohet, 1989). Supervision can be costly for schools in terms of time and staff development for supervisor training. However, the benefits to be reaped if supervision is done well are in ensuring continued tutor health and fitness for purpose. Supervision challenges the tutor to see the pastoral role as a continuous learning process, questioning assumptions and beliefs about relationships and stretching the tutor to clarify the difference between his or her own issues for development and that of the pupils. It also challenges pastoral leaders to devise opportunities for tutors to attend in a managed, structural way to their own emotional agendas.

Peer support groups are an alternative to the supervisor system. Such groups have the advantage of being immediate, free, self-help systems and the contract for such a group can be worked out by the members themselves. They can provide a useful sounding board for individuals to voice their distress and relieve work-related stress. Farber (1983) points to a growing body of research evidence which indicates the efficacy of such groups as a vehicle for combating teacher stress and burn-out. They have the advantage of being non-managerial, so that the members of the group have no lurking fantasies about the motives of other members. The function of such a group is not to provide a mutual moan session but to allow its members to discharge feelings and be listened to sensitively. The group might decide for itself to become action orientated rather than listening orientated, if this is the preference of the members, and usefully discuss strategies for dealing with current dilemmas. The idea of peer support groups for pastoral teams could be initiated by pastoral leaders as a means of legitimately flagging up the necessity for tutors to have a time and place to talk about key issues. However, the decision about numbers and membership of such groups should be left to individuals to negotiate and should be entirely voluntary.

Mentoring, or what Americans sometimes call the 'buddy-system', is another variation on institutional support, but one which does not require extensive training. Mentors are usually designated members of staff, who are generally recognized to have a high level of interpersonal functioning and have the trust and respect of colleagues. They may be experienced or senior members of staff, but this is not essential. What is essential is the willingness to offer a supportive, developmental relationship which will display aspects of both guidance and counselling (Watts, 1986). Contracts for the mentor–mentee relationship again can be negotiated to suit the individuals. Issues brought to the relationship by the mentee are drawn from their professional role and it is completely legitimate to talk about the feelings generated by interpersonal encounters with pupils or staff. It is possible to envisage a school pastoral system where every tutor was both a mentor and a mentee.

CONCLUDING THOUGHTS

Pastoral care is at the very heart of the school as a learning community because it challenges us as teachers to continue to make sense of our own lives and experience, before we have the humility (or temerity) to support our pupils' social and emotional as well as academic development. Teachers who are really life-long learners retain the capacity to empathize with pupils engaged in the struggle to learn. However pastoral care finds expression in schools, it challenges us to explore ways of supporting each other on a tangible day-to-day basis. We can begin to do this by acknowledging at an institutional level the leadership challenge to create and sustain supportive networks for pastoral tutors to develop their emotional intelligence through planned supervision, mentoring or peer support groups. Teachers' relationships with themselves and the quality of their own personal lives will either expand or diminish their capacity to be the kind of teacher who can most consistently and valuably contribute to the development of the pupils in their care.

REFERENCES

Abaci, R., Hall, E. and Hall, C. (1997) *The Effects of Human Relations Training on Teacher Stress, Locus of Control and Pupil Control Ideology*. BJEP (in press).

Aspey, R., Hall, E. and Hall, C. (1976) *A Lever Long Enough*. Dallas: National Consortium for Humanizing Education.

Best, R., Lang, P., Lodge, C. and Watkins, C. (eds) (1995) *Pastoral Care and Personal-Social Education*. London: Cassell.

Bond, T. (1990) Counselling-supervision – ethical issues. *Counselling*, **1**(2), 43–6.

Bowes, M. (1988) Short courses in human relations. *British Journal of In-Service Education*, **14**(2), 75–80.

California Task Force To Promote Self-Esteem and Social Responsibility (1990) Final Report.

Egan, G. (1994) *The Skilled Helper*. Pacific Grove, CA: Brooks/Cole.

Farber, B. A. (ed.) (1983) *Stress and Burnout in the Human Service Professions*. New York: Pergamon Press.

Goleman, D. (1996) *Emotional Intelligence: Why It Can Matter More Than I.Q.* London: Bloomsbury.

Hall, E. and Hall, C. (1988) *Human Relations in Education*. London: Routledge.

Hargreaves, A. and Fullan, M. J. (eds) (1992) *Understanding Teacher Development*. New York: Cassell.

Hawkins, P. and Shohet, R. (1989) *Supervision in the Helping Professions*. Milton Keynes: Open University Press.

Kabat-Zinn, J. (1996) *Full Catastrophe Living*. London: Piatkus.

Kottler, J. A. and Kottler, E. (1993) *Teacher as Counsellor*. CA: Corwin Press.

McGuiness, J. (1989) *A Whole-School Approach to Pastoral Care*. London: Kogan Page.

Mahoney, M. J. (1991) *Human Change Processes*. New York: Basic Books.

Maslow, A. (1954) *Motivation and Personality*. New York: Harper and Row.

O'Connell, A. and O'Connell, V. (1980) *Choice and Change*. Englewood Cliffs: Prentice-Hall.

Palmer, S., Dainow, S. and Milner, P. (eds) (1996) *The BAC Counselling Reader*. London: Sage.

Reasoner, R. and Dusa, G. (1991) *Building Self-Esteem in the Secondary School*. Palo Alto, CA: Consulting Psychologists Press.

Rogers, C. (1962) The interpersonal relationship: the core of guidance. *Harvard Educational Review*, **32**(4).

Rogers, C. (1963) The concept of the fully-functioning person. *Psychotherapy: Theory, Research, and Practice*, **1**(1), 17–26.

Rogers, C. (1980) *A Way of Being*. Boston: Houghton Mifflin.

Rogers, C. and Freiberg, H. J. (1994) *Freedom to Learn*. New York: Merrill.

Scott Peck, M. (1993) *Further Along the Road Less Travelled*. London: Simon and Schuster.

Thorne, B. (1985) *The Quality of Tenderness*. Norwich: Norwich Centre Publications.

Watts, A. G. (1986) Mentoring. *Counselling*, **57**, 4–7.

CHAPTER 4

Managing pastoral care with masculinity in mind

Alan Skelton

So today, boys are trying to turn themselves into men through smashing things up, hanging around in a menacing way, being 'hard', not listening to adult voices, joy-riding, looking for a fight all the time ... breaking into places, and burning community buildings down, often schools. The unofficial syllabus of the streets is about learning how to be a 'real man' for many of these boys. (Jackson and Salisbury, 1996, p. 103)

We were talking about whether in general, women brought different ways of managing to school management .... Suddenly the group fell silent, and it was as though the same puzzling look passed across all their faces ... they explained very patiently to me that leading schools was such an awful job that they were very happy to leave it to men, and to those few women who wanted to do it. School management, as constructed in Britain at the moment, is framed within a very male discourse of the market place, competition, hierarchy, finance and inspection. (Gold, 1994, p. 4)

INTRODUCTION

In this chapter I want to argue that the management of pastoral care in secondary schools urgently needs to address the problem of masculinity in schools and wider society; a problem which is escalating and which has implications for management decisions about *what* a pastoral care curriculum might include, *how* it is to be organized and *who* will take responsibility for its co-ordination. One only has to scan the newspapers to get a sense of what is at stake. The rising tide of disruptive behaviour in schools and the fearful calls for school security against male attack are suggestive of a rising social problem. It would seem that many boys prefer to 'mess about' and intimidate others rather than engage with their school work. A recent study carried out by OFSTED and the Equal Opportunities Commission showed that girls are now more successful than boys at every level in GCSE, with more achieving at least one grade G and more passing five subjects at grade C or above (Carvel, 1996). As one boy was reported to say in a recent *Times Magazine* article: 'You can't win. If you answer the question wrong then you're jeered at for being stupid and if you answer right then you're a boffin or a swot or a brainbox' (Wheatley, 1996, pp. 18–19).

The behaviour of many men in school is also a cause for concern. Studies show that male teacher sexual harassment of female pupils and teachers in classrooms and staffrooms is commonplace (Jones, 1985; Mahony, 1989). Male violence is also an accepted if covert part of secondary school life with many men routinely using verbal threats and/or physical force (e.g. hitting, pushing and shaking) to coerce boys into 'appropriate' forms of behaviour (Beynon, 1989). Men's management of secondary schools is equally problematic. Men dominate school management (Equal Opportunities Commission, 1995), yet they have done little to challenge the values implicit in the management models assumed and required by the Education Reform Act. Under the guise of contemporary school 'management', men distance themselves from the implications their behaviour has for the lives of other people. In the interests of curriculum 'efficiency', 'coherence' and 'structure', men are prepared to 'tough it out': making those 'difficult' decisions that terminate contracts, 'lose' loyal part-timers and move staff into positions they are not trained for.

Up until recently, secondary schools have ignored issues to do with masculinity. They have been prepared to devote considerable amounts of time, energy and resources to boys' misbehaviour and have put up with the negative implications boys' and men's behaviour has for school 'climate' and 'ethos'. Many schools are now wanting to challenge this unacceptable state of affairs. A carefully managed pastoral programme which addresses issues to do with masculinity can promote positive behaviours in boys and men which will clearly benefit the whole school community.

THE CRISIS OF MASCULINITY

Male behaviour in school might be explained by what is often termed in the literature the 'crisis of masculinity'. This crisis has arisen as traditional ways of understanding what it means to be a boy or a man in our society have become increasingly difficult to sustain, leading to uncertainty and confusion. For example, the traditional bread-winner role has all but vanished with more than 20 per cent of men now having female partners who are the household's main earners – a threefold rise since the early 1980s (Cohen, 1996). Traditional male areas of employment such as mining, shipbuilding and the steel industry have also all but disappeared, and many new jobs which are being created are in female-dominated service industries. Men's health seems to be suffering in the light of these social changes. Recent figures show a significant deterioration in the well-being of men compared to women. For example, men die six years younger than women and are four times more likely to commit suicide, possibly because they find it difficult to seek advice or help from therapeutic processes (O'Brien, 1990). A recent report from the Royal College of Psychiatrists (April 1996) summed up the growing malaise by stating that the modern man is quite simply 'depressed' (see Cohen, 1996).

It is important to note that it is not just 'working-class' men who feel uncertain about their masculinity. Men of the professional middle class who have traditionally displayed their prowess through intellectual (as opposed to physical) power and control (see Connell, 1989) are also under threat. Economic recession, the accompanying rise of the short-term contract and increased demands by women for equal contributions to domestic responsibilities, all mean that the professional man can no longer expect to progress cleanly up the career ladder and rely on the 'woman at home' to look after the children and do the housework. Despite the potential opportunities that feminism has opened up for men and although there have been tentative noises made about the 'New Man', there appears to be little change on the ground. In fact, if one considers the xenophobic and racist hooliganism evident in the 1996 European Soccer Championships after the game with Germany and men's continued physical and sexual attacks on women and other men (see Miles, 1992, pp. 11–14), then the situation, if anything, appears to be getting worse. Frosh (1995, p. 222) helps to explain this seemingly paradoxical state of affairs by suggesting that 'as traditional modes of masculinity become harder to sustain, so, in the absence of other, fuller sources of identity, it is clung to more desperately'.

PASTORAL CARE AND GENDER ISSUES

The need to eradicate sexism and provide genuine equal opportunities cannot easily be separated from a school's overall responsibility for the personal and social development of its pupils.

(Lang and Ribbins, 1991, p. vii)

While gender has been readily identified as either a fundamental component of pastoral care or one form of social inequality within which pastoral care needs to be defined and expressed (see Leicester, 1990, for work which considers the relationship between pastoral care and anti-racist education), there have been surprisingly few books and articles which have addressed the relationship between pastoral care and gender issues and little policy development in this area. One notable exception is the book *Gender and Pastoral Care* by McLaughlin *et al.* (1991) which offered guidance on how a pastoral care policy might integrate gender concerns as a central organizing theme. This book was particularly timely in the light of the National Curriculum's expressed commitment to equal opportunities (EOPs) as one of its major cross-curricular dimensions and offered concrete ways of applying this policy to practice. In accordance with many educationalists working in the pastoral care field at that time, the book took the line that gender – like pastoral care itself – should ideally be a whole school issue which needed to be addressed by all staff and by all school subjects, rather than purely by pastoral care specialists in discrete Personal and Social Education (PSE) lessons. Gender was identified as a pervasive feature of school life both in and outside classrooms; attention being drawn to boys' domination of playground and corridor space and their use of such spaces to intimidate girls (and women teachers). Gender was also seen to be a central part of the 'hidden curriculum' of schooling; the chapter by Lodge (1991) discusses ways in which gender stereotypes influence classroom interaction, individual casework and teacher reports of pupil progress and contribute to the subsequent restricted life and career opportunities available to women.

THE LIMITATIONS OF AN EOPs APPROACH TO GENDER WORK

The EOPs approach adopted in *Gender and Pastoral Care* characterizes much of the gender work that took place in secondary schools in the 1970s and 1980s. This work focused on empowering girls and women by drawing attention to boys' control over mixed-sex classrooms, the male bias inherent in curriculum materials and male teachers' greater access to positions of responsibility and decision-making structures in schools (for example, see Stanworth, 1981; Walkerdine, 1981; Cornbleet and Libovitch, 1983; Beecham, 1983). While it is crucially important to continue this work, it needs to be supplemented by an approach which may be more suited to the current understandings, needs, experiences and feelings of boys and men (Salisbury and Jackson, 1996). In the light of recent theoretical developments which stress the importance of thinking about *masculinities* rather than simply masculinity (see Mac An Ghaill, 1996; Hearn, 1996), such an approach would need to focus on *differences* in and between boys and in and between men as a basis for change. It would seek to build on previous EOPs gender work by acknowledging that there is an overarching power-relation between boys/girls and men/women in society, but that within this power-relation, not *all* boys/men act in the same controlling ways with some acting for the promotion of anti-oppressive relations and practices. A *particular* boy's or man's behaviour may also change depending on the time, place or context he finds himself in; in other words, it is too simplistic to talk of an undifferentiated boy or man's behaviour that is simply played out irrespective of situations, moments and intentions. (Note that from this point on I will adopt singular categories such as 'boys' or 'girls' rather than boys/men and girls/women to make the text easier to follow. In doing this I will assume that the reader recognizes that I will often be implicitly referring to both child and adult categories as they are both implicated in large parts of the discussion.)

Differences in and between men, however small, open up possibilities for change and focusing on them is a more positive enabling strategy than concentrating on the negative aspects of men's behaviour. Working with differences does not seek to 'wrestle the initiative' away from women to men like some of the more reactionary, anti-feminist writings that are beginning to appear as part of the current concern for and interest in men (e.g. Lyndon, 1996). Nor is it an example of an educational approach which seeks to raise boys' achievement without any due regard for broader questions of masculinity – an approach evident in a number of recent writings on boys in secondary schools (e.g. Woodhead, 1996).

Rather, it serves to supplement gender work with girls and to encourage a commitment to anti-sexist behaviour and practice in boys.

WORKING WITH DIFFERENCE: BOYS AND MASCULINITY

Within the secondary school context, what might a 'working with difference' approach look like and how might it be managed? The first thing to say here is that such work – like pastoral care itself – needs to be conceived as a whole school concern rather than tucked away simply as part of PSE or form tutor time. It is important to stress, however, that pastoral care managers (such as senior teachers with pastoral care responsibilities, middle managers such as year heads and PSE co-ordinators) may be well placed to support and act as *advocates* for such a whole school approach and to raise awareness of the need for masculinity issues to be addressed as part of a school's pastoral programme. This will require sensitivity to the insecurities of some male teachers who are likely to fear (and therefore oppose) any gender work and masculinity work in particular. It will also require a sensitivity to both men and women who have internalized the neo-conservative attacks on 'political correctness' that have recently encouraged people to see equity work of any kind (e.g. race, gender, disability, etc.) as coming from fanatics (Richer and Weir, 1995). In responding to these sensitivities, it is important to remember that one of the undoubted strengths of a 'working with difference' approach is its positive nature. This, together with the potential pay-offs for teachers in terms of reduced disaffection and increased motivation from boys, are two powerful incentives for adopting a whole school approach to gender work which would identify masculinity as an urgent and particular aspect of this work which supplements initiatives with girls.

In addition to playing an advocate role, pastoral care managers will need to have a clear *understanding* of the types of school activities that might contribute to masculinity work and the purpose(s) of such work. PSE sessions are an appropriate place for the exploration of issues such as violence and bullying, sexual harassment, sexuality, sport, relationships, the media and language (see Salisbury and Jackson, 1996). But school subjects are also places where such issues may be addressed and differences in opinion, experience and expectation between boys can be identified and discussed. Martino (1995), for example, demonstrates how the English classroom can be used as a focus for work on masculinities. He describes the reactions of 40 adolescent boys to a story 'The Altar of the Family' by Michael Wilding (see Keyte and Baines, 1982). In the story a boy shoots a possum after his father – who has seen the boy playing with his sister's dolls – suggests he may turn into a 'lily-livered poofter'. Martino asked the boys to write a response to the story, offering them an opportunity 'to question, challenge and reflect upon' (p. 212) the implicit meanings about masculinity carried within it. While none of the boys questioned the underlying assumption that playing with dolls signifies that you are unmanly or homosexual, 36 out of 40 of them clearly rejected the way the father treated the son. They did so for a variety of reasons with some focusing on the bullying behaviour of the father and others identifying with the boy's sense of isolation which triggered the shooting. This work demonstrates how the subject of masculinity – evoked here through discussions about father–son relations – can be opened up in English lessons to allow possibilities for boys to explore their emerging feelings and opinions. Work in other subject areas might follow a similar line with biology courses, for example, addressing the issue of whether male violence is instinctive or socially constructed to maintain male power and privilege in society (Salisbury and Jackson, 1996). Again the purpose here would be to open up issues of masculinity and to explore the differing responses of boys. Similar planned and co-ordinated responses from within or across other curriculum areas would serve to 'flesh out' notions of working with difference or *inter-cultural articulation* which have been put forward in the literature as a guiding principle for masculinity work in inner-city schools (Walker, 1988) and in specific areas of the secondary school curriculum (Skelton, 1993).

A 'working with difference' approach with boys might therefore seek to combine separately timetabled PSE slots (which would primarily use single-sex work) with subject-based work on masculinity. This would require careful orchestration with pastoral/PSE, subject-based curriculum and EOPs co-ordinators working together to ensure an effective programme (see Lodge, 1995).

WORKING WITH DIFFERENCE: MEN, MANAGEMENT AND MASCULINITY

A consideration of the relationship between pastoral care and masculinity cannot overlook *man*agement itself, as if management is something which is given that simply 'delivers' a pastoral programme. Management in secondary schools is inherently problematic, as is the management of pastoral care. As stated at the very beginning of this chapter, management in secondary schools is currently framed within a very male discourse of the market-place, competition, hierarchy, finance and inspection (Gold, 1994). This hardly corresponds with contemporary discourses about what pastoral care means and seeks to achieve in secondary schools: namely a *caring* community (Stoll and Fink, 1996) which is concerned with *people* (see Harrison, Chapter 1). A body of work on alternative models of management and leadership appeared in the 1970s and 1980s principally through feminist scholarship. A different approach to management was articulated which emphasized collaboration, participation through building relationships, sharing information and valuing the views and contributions of all organizational members (Court, 1994; Shakeshaft, 1989). Despite this work, the principal management model that currently prevails in secondary schools in Britain and in many other countries is an inappropriate business model. This model has gradually evolved in the light of the requirements of the ERA and its underlying rationale is industrial productivity and market competition (Ball, 1990).

Pastoral care management cannot ignore this state of affairs. It is a contradiction of massive proportions to 'manage' pastoral care simply by concentrating on how a set of organizational structures might deliver a given pastoral programme; pastoral care management requires those concerned to think about management *itself* and how it serves to under-mine the very basis of pastoral care work in schools. In other words, the concept of management needs to be problematized and the masculine basis of dominant conceptualizations needs to be opened up for discussion and scrutiny. An effective pastoral care programme in secondary schools would therefore need to address the relationship between management and masculinity as part of its attempt to foster an ethos of care and community. 'Macho management' (see Court, 1994) which 'stresses hier-archy, structured roles and functions and motivation driven by com-petition and individualism' (ibid., p. 33) therefore needs to be questioned in the light of the potentially harmful effects it may have on personal relations which are the lifeblood of any school community. Male man-agers need to be given opportunities to explore *differences* between them in the way they conceptualize, experience and carry out management tasks. Alternative approaches to leadership and management (such as feminist models) would be useful to consider here as part of such explorations, in order to break down the myth that there is 'only one way to manage'. Sharing differences in experience may also challenge many men's assumption that there is only one *real* way for *men* to manage.

Male pastoral care managers potentially have important contributions to make to a 'working with difference' approach of this kind. In compar-ison to managers of hard-edged, academic subjects, pastoral care man-agers work in what has historically been perceived to be a 'soft', 'feminine' area which focuses, as was mentioned earlier, on people and caring. The requirements that pastoral care brings to management would therefore appear to offer opportunities for the articulation of a different approach to management: namely one that challenges the dominant masculinist form. Slade (1991), however, points to the difficulties in adopting a different approach to managing pastoral care in contemporary secondary schools given the shortage of resources and the need to compete for them:

Key pastoral care staff are usually selected because they possess certain virtues; these include patience, kindness and a willingness to see both sides of an argument. But from the point of view of ensuring a sound management of pastoral care, these virtues can be their own undoing. One might argue that as long as pastoral care staff demonstrate in management all the virtues which make them so valuable when dealing with children, then children themselves will be the recipients of a confused and inefficient service. (Slade, 1991, p. 46)

While there are a number of examples where pastoral care seems to be encouraging a different approach to management (for example, by 'flat-tening' top-down management structures through the creation of new middle-management posts – see Megahy, Chapter 2 above), the perceived femininity of pastoral care might conversely encourage its managers to overcompensate by becoming the *most* masculine of the managers in secondary schools. There is some research evidence to suggest that given the control emphasis in the 'first phase' of pastoral care in the late 1960s and 1970s (Bulman and Jenkins, 1988), its middle managers (heads of year, heads of house, heads of lower and upper school) were appointed on the basis of them being 'super disciplinarians' (Bell and Maher, 1986).

Since this period, a considerable body of research and development work has been carried out in relation to pastoral care which now tends to be defined in broader terms, emphasizing both the responsibilities and *rights* of all individuals within the school community (Best, 1989). Despite the optimism of 'stage theories' of pastoral care's evolution, however, which stress its development and refinement (e.g. from an emphasis on control to an emphasis on developing people in the school), experiences 'on the ground' often suggest there has been little movement. The illustrative case study of Les Newton in the book by Salisbury and Jackson (1996, pp. 23–5) suggests that pastoral care management might not have progressed as far as we might think. Les is the head of lower school at an East Midlands inner-city comprehensive who has a deputy, Marjorie Etherington. Their behaviour is gendered in that Les is clearly the 'aggressive, hard disciplinary person' in the pastoral partnership whereas Marjorie is the 'caring' one. In the following short extract taken from the book, Les approaches the school hall:

On another occasion, some Year 7 boys were waiting to go into the hall for a dance lesson. They were showing themselves to be keen and eager to get in and start. Les Newton passed them and commented on their enthusiasm by giving a limp wrist, 'camp' gesture. In view of the prevalent homophobic atmosphere around the school, what should boys be thinking about themselves in relation to dance in the eyes of the head of lower school? What a clear message is contained in this signal to boys since, according to the behaviour of the head of lower school, dance has no place in boys' lives if they are considered to be *real boys*. (Salisbury and Jackson, 1996, p. 24. My italics)

It is perhaps tempting to see Les Newton as a one-off; a man who is not representative of the broader base of male pastoral care managers. If one remembers, however, that most of the EOPs work that was carried out in schools in the 1970s and 1980s focused on *pupils* rather than staff, it is not difficult to appreciate that many male teachers and managers in schools have not really needed to seriously address issues about their masculinity to date. Part of the problem here is the assumption that pastoral care work of any kind – gender related or not – concerns pupils not staff.

As I have argued elsewhere, pupils will not take pastoral care seriously if its values are not applied to teachers and reflected in the way they behave (Skelton, 1991). Any 'whole school' notion of pastoral care surely has to include the pastoral needs of *staff* and to challenge the male *distancing from self* that a focus on pupils assumes and requires (see Hall, ch. 3). Of course staff members are not a homogeneous group who exist in a social and school context which is 'gender-free'. Staff development work for teachers needs to urgently address gender issues and much of this work may be best carried out in single-sex groups. Part of it might involve men working in all-male groups to address issues to do with masculinity (e.g. relationships at work; career; stress; anger; the work/home boundary). Development work of this kind with male members of staff might act as a basis for male managers (of pastoral care and other areas of responsibility) to discuss differences in the way in which they conceptualize, experience and implement management tasks in secondary schools. These discussions might also look at differences in the reasons why men chose to become managers, whether expectations of management have been borne out in reality and what implications school management has for other areas of men's lives. Separate gender work for women managers might address the dilemma referred to by Gold (1994) at the beginning of this chapter. Women are currently under-represented in secondary school management and also in 'feminine' areas of management such as pastoral care (HMI, 1990). Does this matter? Do women want to increase their representation in male-defined school management? Change the way management is defined? Or leave it to men since there are other more important things in life?

CONCLUSION

In this chapter I have addressed three practical issues relating to the management of pastoral care in secondary schools: (1) *What* needs to be managed? (Questions to do with pastoral care programmes and curricula); (2) *How* do we manage it? (Questions to do with management itself) and (3) *Who* manages? (Questions to do with personnel). I have argued that the current crisis in masculinity provides an important social context within which such questions have to be framed, understood and responded to by those involved in pastoral care management. For example, in thinking about *what* needs to be managed, I have argued that it is timely for pastoral care to address the issue of how boys and men behave in schools which has detrimental effects on others (and themselves) and which undermines the school as a community. I have also argued that in addressing issues to do with *how* to manage, current conceptualizations of management which are underpinned by dominant versions of masculinity need to be opened up for discussion and alternatives, such as feminist approaches, considered. In respect of the third question – *who* manages – I have argued that the limitations of control-focused 'super disciplinarians' and homophobics such as Les Newton need to be recognized and more appropriate personnel considered: namely men and women who have an understanding of the responsibilities and *rights* of pupils and who value other members of the school community irrespective of their gender, race, social class, sexual orientation and/or disability.

Running through the chapter is the theme of 'working with difference'. In the light of recent theoretical work which suggests we should view masculinity as a heterogeneous concept, this theme has been articulated in each of the three practical questions posed. Central to the theme is the idea that boys and men should be encouraged to explore differences between them in terms of ideas, feelings and experiences in order to break down the restrictions and self-destructive sets of behaviours that dominant versions of masculinity can encourage. Part of the problem is the myth of a 'monolithic' masculinity (Siedler, 1991): the assumption held by most men that *other* men act in a coherent, unified and 'manly' way. A pastoral care programme in secondary schools can play an important role in breaking down this myth by encouraging men, including male pastoral care managers, to share experience and consider alternative ways of behaving. This can only help challenge the destructive effects of male behaviour in secondary schools and open up possibilities for a greater range of satisfying ways of being in the world and relating to other people.

REFERENCES

Ball, S. J. (1990) Markets, inequality and urban schooling. *The Urban Review*, **22**, 85–100.

Beecham, Y. (1983) Women's studies and beyond – the feminisation of education. *GEN*, **1** (Autumn).

Bell, L. and Maher, P. (1986) *Leading a Pastoral Team*. Oxford: Blackwell.

Best, R. E. (1989) Pastoral care: some reflections and a restatement. *Pastoral Care in Education*, **7**(4), 7–13.

Beynon, J. (1989) A school for men: an ethnographic case study of routine violence in schooling. In Walker, S. and Barton. L. (eds) *Politics and the Processes of Schooling*. Milton Keynes: Open University Press.

Bulman, L. and Jenkins, D. (1988) *The Pastoral Curriculum*. Oxford: Blackwell.

Carvel, J. (1996) Schools urged to focus on low achieving boys. *The Guardian*, 11 July.

Cohen, D. (1996) It's a guy thing. *The Guardian*, 4 May.

Connell, R. W. (1989) Cool guys, swots and wimps: the interplay of masculinity and education. *Oxford Review of Education*, **15**(3), 291–303.

Cornbleet, A. and Libovitch, S. (1983) Anti-sexist initiatives in a mixed comprehensive school: a case study. In Wolpe, A. M. and Donald, J. (eds) *Is There Anyone Here From Education?* London: Pluto Press.

Court, M. (1994) Removing macho management: lessons from the field of education. *Gender, Work and Organization*, **1**(1), 33–49.

Equal Opportunities Commission (1995) *Some Facts About Women – 1995, Great Britain*. Manchester: Equal Opportunities Commission.

Frosh, S. (1995) Unpacking masculinity: from rationality to fragmentation. In Burck, C. and Speed, B. (eds) *Gender, Power and Relationships*. London: Routledge.

Gold, A. (1994) Working with silences: planning management development programmes which work for women too. Paper presented at The European Network for Improving Research and Development in Educational Management, Majvik, Finland. 29 September–2 October.

Hearn, J. (1996) Is masculinity dead? A critique of the concept of masculinity/masculinities. In Mac An Ghaill, M. (ed.) *Understanding Masculinities*. Buckingham: Open University Press.

Her Majesty's Inspectorate (HMI) (1990) *Pastoral Care in Secondary Schools: An Inspection of Some Aspects of Pastoral Care in 1987–1988*. London: DES.

Jackson, D. and Salisbury, J. (1996) Why should secondary schools take working with boys seriously? *Gender and Education*, **8**(1), 103–15.

Jones, C. (1985) Sexual tyranny in mixed schools. In Weiner, G. (ed.) *Just a Bunch of Girls*. Milton Keynes: Open University Press.

Keyte, B. and Baines, R. (eds) (1982) *The Loaded Dice: A Short Anthology*. Melbourne: Nelson.

Lang, P. and Ribbins, P. (1991) Preface. In McLaughlin, C., Lodge, C. and Watkins, C. (eds) *Gender and Pastoral Care*. Oxford: Blackwell.

Leicester, M. (1990) Pastoral care and anti-racist education: interface and synthesis – preliminary remarks. *Pastoral Care in Education*, 8(1), 2–4.

Lodge, C. (1991) Gender, pastoral care and the whole school: policy and action. In McLaughlin, C., Lodge, C. and Watkins, C. *Gender and Pastoral Care*. Oxford: Blackwell.

Lodge, C. (1995) School management for pastoral care and PSE. In Best, R. *et al.* (eds) *Pastoral Care and Personal-Social Education: Entitlement and Provision*. London: Cassell.

Lyndon, N. (1996) Man trouble. *The Guardian*, 14 May.

Mac An Ghaill, M. (ed.) (1996) *Understanding Masculinities*. Buckingham: Open University Press.

McLaughlin, C., Lodge, C. and Watkins, C. (1991) *Gender and Pastoral Care*. Oxford: Blackwell.

Mahony, P. (1989) Sexual violence in mixed schools. In Jones, C. and Mahony, P. (eds) *Learning Our Lines: Sexuality and Social Control in Education*. London: The Women's Press.

Martino, W. (1995) Deconstructing masculinity in the English classroom: a site for reconstituting gendered subjectivity. *Gender and Education*, 7(2), 205–20.

Miles, R. (1992) *The Rites of Man*. London: Paladin.

O'Brien, M. (1990) The place of men in a gender-sensitive therapy. In Perleberg, R. J. and Miller, A. (eds) *Gender and Power in Families*. London: Routledge.

Richer, S. and Weir, L. (eds) (1995) *Beyond Political Correctness: Toward the Inclusive University*. Toronto: University of Toronto Press.

Salisbury, J. and Jackson, D. (1996) *Challenging Macho Values: Practical Ways of Working with Adolescent Boys*. London: Falmer Press.

Shakeshaft, C. (1989) *Women in Educational Administration*. London: Sage.

Siedler, V. (1991) *Recreating Sexual Politics*. London: Routledge.

Skelton, A. (1991) Don't I matter, too? Pastoral needs of staff in educational institutions. *Pastoral Care in Education*, 9(4), 3–5.

Skelton, A. (1993) On becoming a male physical education teacher: the informal culture of students and the construction of hegemonic masculinity. *Gender and Education*, 5(3), 289–303.

Slade, T.(1991) Changing pastoral roles: a case of overloading? *Pastoral Care in Education*, 9(4), 45–6.

Stanworth, M. (1981) *Gender and Schooling: A Study of Sexual Divisions in the Classroom*. London: WRRC.

Stoll, L. and Fink, D. (1996) *Changing Our Schools: Linking School Effectiveness and School Improvement*. Buckingham: Open University Press.

Walker, J. C. (1988) The way men act: dominant and subordinate male cultures in an inner-city school. *British Journal of Sociology of Education*, 9(1), 3–18.

Walkerdine, V. (1981) Sex, power and pedagogy. *Science Education*, **38** (Spring).

Wheatley, J. (1996) Outclassed. *The Times Magazine*, 30 March.

Woodhead, C. (1996) Boys who learn to be losers. *The Times*, 6 March.

CHAPTER 5

Managing inter-agency support
Mike Calvert, Geoff Evans and Jenny Henderson

INTRODUCTION

Inter-agency support, like pastoral care itself, has been a victim of piecemeal development (Craft, 1980) over the years. The result is a complex patchwork of services with their own practices, traditions, prejudices, conflicting interests and problems. Craft highlights the complexity of the range and pattern of provision and presents an uneven picture both in terms of different schools in an authority and across Local Education Authorities (LEAs). This chapter attempts to present an up-to-date picture that takes into account changes that have occurred since the 1980s and which, without doubt, present schools with even greater challenges and responsibilities.

A recurrent theme of the whole book is the need to manage rather than let things happen. This chapter presents a picture of a system in crisis, where dedicated professionals are forced into reactive roles, having to make hard choices when prioritizing, so as to either comply with statutory legislation and/or simply survive in a market-driven education system. The result is a position that threatens to increase the inequality of provision and to present some schools and communities with impossible challenges. Although the picture might well be bleak in places, the aim is not to depress the reader but to argue that this calls for even greater efforts and management skills to implement strategies, to adopt, where possible, proactive, preventative measures. They must harness intelligently the resources and expertise from outside if the needs of more of our pupils are to be met. 'All successful management is about getting the most from existing resources' (Solity and Bickler, 1994) but, it will be argued, schools cannot do everything on their own.

The chapter begins by looking at some of the changes that have taken place: changes in legislation, in society and in the organization of the education system that put in context the issues that professionals in the field of education have to face in the late 1990s. It goes on to focus on the work of two schools and the agencies that work with them. The authors highlight issues that arise from the case studies and make some positive recommendations as to how schools might move forward.

The schools are situated in two different Northern (post-)industrial cities. The schools were chosen because they both call upon outside agencies a great deal and are making active efforts to forge links with these agencies and with community groups in order to improve the welfare of the children in their care and to enhance the image of the school. There is no such thing as a typical school and there is no suggestion that the schools chosen for the case study represent typical comprehensive schools. It is expected, however, that readers will identify with many of the issues and problems that the schools and agencies face and we believe that especially in urban and/or disadvantaged areas the picture is not an unfamiliar one.

In preparing the chapter we were able to interview a range of professionals who work with School A and, in the case of School B, interview the head and a deputy. It could be argued that we have omitted to mention potentially the most important outside agency – the parents. We have chosen to restrict our focus to formal agencies and would refer readers to Tomlinson's chapter on home–school links in Best *et al.* (1995) for a detailed treatment of the subject.

THE CONTEXT

We begin by stressing changes that have taken place in recent years and highlighting new challenges that teachers and managers face. Societal shifts, new legislation and changes in administration and funding all add to teachers' responsibilities and, at times, call into question the schools' ability to cope.

Pastoral demands on staff have increased dramatically as pupils bring more social and emotional problems to school. Hutton (1996) and Maden (1996) present a disturbing picture of growing social inequality with poverty and unemployment being increasingly unfairly distributed. The divorce rate is increasing (Desforges, 1995) and the subsequent fragmentation of family life is all too common. In terms of abuse, society has been slow to recognize or admit to its existence and extent, as the Cleveland Report (1988) illustrates.

Young people, too, are changing. They mature more quickly, are sexually active from an earlier age and, as Whitney (1994) points out, 'many pupils live lifestyles outside school hours which reflect a culture previously available only to adults'. They are 'significant consumers' (ibid.) targeted by the media and advertising. A disturbing number have domestic and caring responsibilities.

In terms of legislation, schools have been bombarded with change. The Education Reform Act (1988) heralded the arrival of the National Curriculum and altered the role of the LEAs. Their role and influence have since declined as resources have been devolved to schools through Local Management of Schools (LMS) and they face an uncertain future (Russell, 1992). This is particularly threatening in the light of recent government moves for all schools to opt out of local government control and the threat of inspections of LEAs. Both of these measures are likely to further call into question their very nature and existence. Prior to this, the 1981 Education Act, in the light of the Warnock Committee report, called for the integration of pupils with special educational needs, which led to the closure of many special schools. The procedures for identifying and addressing the special needs of pupils was strengthened by the Code of Practice (DfE, 1994).

Of direct importance to multi-agency co-operation is the 1989 Children Act. The Act is wide-ranging and has significant implications for pastoral care provision (Hodgson and Whalley, 1992) especially with reference to 'children in need' (not to be confused with children with special needs). In section 17, two categories are identified: the child who has a disability and the child who 'is unlikely to achieve or maintain, or to have the opportunity of achieving or maintaining, a reasonable standard of health or development without the provision for him (sic) of services by a local authority' (quoted in Hodgson and Whalley, 1992, p. 20). The Act calls for agencies to work together (see Home Office et al., 1991). Significantly, the Act (cf. Section 27, 'Co-operation between authorities') says nothing about how this co-operation is to be translated into practice (Hodgson and Whalley, 1992). Working practices 'have all been based around a model of inter-agency provision rather than each adopting a narrow perspective of their own' (Whitney, 1994, p. 68). The Act, which came into force in 1991, states the requirement that each school has to have a Child Protection Liaison Officer and DfEE *Circular 10/95* sets out the duties of the designated officer in schools and what teachers should know. OFSTED (1995) refers, in a number of places, to links with other organizations, highlighting the role of parents. Referring to special educational needs, they state that schools should ensure that 'the use of specialist support from outside agencies is well managed within the school' (p. 113).

THE SCHOOLS AND THE AGENCIES

School A
School A is an 11–16 state comprehensive school with 1150 pupils on roll. It is on a split site and is situated in a disadvantaged area of the city with high levels of social deprivation and unemployment. In all, 45 per cent of pupils are eligible for free school meals (generally considered in the UK as being a reliable index of economic standing). In terms of ability, non-verbal reasoning tests indicate that 45 per cent of the intake will experience learning difficulties at some stage in their school career. This does not take into account the other needs that pupils will have which will inevitably add to, and compound the effects of, any learning difficulties they might possess. In fact, there are between 500 and 540 pupils on the special needs register; 19 have full statements and 350 are at levels 2 and 3 (Code of Practice, DfE, 1994). Truancy levels are high with 60 per cent of pupils attending less than 90 per cent of the time and only 20 per cent achieve five or more GCSE grades at A–C grade. The intake of the school is influenced negatively by three factors. Firstly, the 11–18 schools in the city are favoured by parents. Secondly, other 11–16 schools in the area are perceived as being better because of their results and their intake. Thirdly, the school has had to absorb a large number of pupils who attended a school which was recently closed.

School B

School B is also a state comprehensive school on a split site. It currently has 1400 pupils on roll, expanding to 1800 when it becomes an 11–18 school in the next academic year. The school is in an area of the city which includes two housing estates, with incidence of economic and social disadvantage and high unemployment (cf. Calvert and Henderson, 1995 for an earlier case study of the school). One-third of the parents are in receipt of benefit and, in two areas from which the pupils are drawn, car ownership stands at 50 per cent. There are approximately 350 pupils on the special needs register and 60 with full statements. Levels of achievement in GCSEs are comparable to those of School A with 23 per cent achieving five or more A–C grade passes. The school is recognized as having a strong pastoral system and acknowledged as coping well with pupils with special needs. It consequently attracts a number of pupils who fall into this category.

The schools, as was stated earlier, are in different cities and are consequently subject to different levels of funding, different support agency systems and individual characteristics which make comparisons both invidious and difficult. Nevertheless, by virtue of the differences between them, it is interesting to look at how the two schools approach work in a number of areas. We begin with Special Educational Needs (SEN).

Both schools face an impossible task with regard to the Code of Practice. Legally they have to provide Individual Education Programmes (IEPs) to all pupils on the special needs register (550 in the case of School A; 350 in the case of School B). The Special Needs Co-ordinator (SENCO) of School A describes it as 'a huge administrative burden with no additional funding'. The deputy of School B refers to a 'virtually unmanageable Code of Practice'. He goes on to add 'No-one would disagree with it in terms of principles, but the practical realities of it are immense'. School A has begun to address the problem by appointing a SENCO at the level of senior curriculum manager. This represents an innovative step in the school and demonstrates a commitment to giving 'priority and high status' to special needs and an attempt to redress the imbalance of so many such pupils in the school. As well as the pupils with learning difficulties, she identifies 'a lot of children who experience extreme behavioural patterns and who regard school as an alien culture' and who do not have parental support. Her role is designed to bring together pastoral and curriculum areas. She describes herself as almost 'an internal outside agency' within the school. She runs a working support team whose role is both consultative and supportive. The system of referrals is, at present, *ad hoc* and she is trying to set up structures for improved communication, reviewing the cases of high priority children. She has also introduced a different system for dealing with serious incidents in the classroom by encouraging collaboration between the special needs department and those responsible for the school's behavioural policy.

Both schools rely heavily on the Education Welfare Officer (EWO) who is involved in addressing problems of attendance and behaviour. In School B the EWO has an office and serves not only the school but the other institutions in the pyramid, which comprises six primary schools and the one secondary school. Being based in the school, the EWO is treated as one of the team, attends staff socials and is, of course, extremely accessible. The EWO has a formal meeting once a week with the heads and assistant heads of year to monitor pupils' progress. Both schools refer to the high workload and stress which, in the case of School B, is seen as contributing to problems of recruitment, temporary appointments, staff turnover and expediency. There is a service-level agreement between the EWO service and the school, which sets down the responsibilities of both parties, but this has been inoperable for most of the year because of staffing problems. In School A, the EWO finds that her caseload is such that she is unable to spend as much time as she would like with families, a growing number of whom are experiencing difficulties in coping for a variety of reasons.

In School B, the school nurse is based in school. The school reports that, because of this, screening has improved and relationships with staff are good. In addition to the services of the nurse, the Local Authority has responded well in the past to special requests for support. Facing the problem of a high rate of student pregnancies, the school was allocated a doctor for one half-day per week to provide a confidential 'drop-in' service. In School A, on the other hand, the nursing sister shares her time with other schools and spends half a day a week in school. Pupils are referred by year tutors or they contact her themselves. She finds that she spends too much time on paperwork and would like to work more with parents on a long-term basis. She would like to see someone 'health-based' in school all the time and be more involved with health education.

Both schools need the services of the Educational Psychologist on a regular basis. Time is rationed in the schools but in different ways. In School A, she visits the school for half a day a fortnight dealing with pupils identified by the school. In School B, there is again a service-level agreement but based on the pyramid of primary and secondary schools as a whole. This provides continuity in the case of families with siblings in the primary sector and a measure of flexibility in the allocation of time. The school sees the service-level agreement as a move forward as, prior to this, they saw very little of the Educational Psychologist and now have 'more on-site time under our control than ever before'. The system is not without its problems, however, since the Educational Psychologist has a heavy caseload which extends to other pyramids and changes of personnel are frequent. The school has considered appointing their own Educational Psychologist, given the need for counselling which is difficult to obtain. In the case of one child whose father is suicidal, the school has been told by one agency that they can only help when there has been a death!

The pressures are apparent in the description by the Educational Psychologist of her work in School A as 'multi-faceted'. She has to identify and assess children's needs and has to support both teachers and pupils. She also has to co-ordinate a multi-agency approach to vulnerable children (e.g. children in the care of the authority and children on the child protection register). She sees the liaison and status of the SEN department as being crucial to her role. She identifies the biggest challenge as the child with behavioural difficulties. IEPs are rare for pupils with such difficulties and she often finds in her work that, when her help is sought, the schools' response has been to follow a disciplinary route – with a sheaf of punishment slips – rather than address the underlying needs of the child. Her other major challenge is catering for the growing number of exclusions. 'There are kids hanging around for longer and getting less.' These pupils are likely to turn to crime and she gives examples of pupils of 14 years old who are in prison. 'Once they're under the criminal justice system everything else goes out of the window. They don't look at other aspects of these children.'

Dealings with Pupil Referral Units (PRUs) reveal an interesting divergence of practice. The Head of Section at the referral centre linked to School A prefers to work with pupils who have been identified as being at risk of being excluded. The school has tried to involve pupils on the fringes of permanent exclusion in the hope of keeping them in school. The School Development Officer has attracted outside funding to organize opportunities for difficult Y10 pupils to have 'time out' with counselling and teaching support. In the case of School B, they report that the PRU dealing with pupils in the 11–14 age range is often full and the pressure comes from the PRUs who would like the school to have their pupils. The school has one pupil who should be placed in the PRU but, as there is not a place for him, he will have to go 'on the permanent exclusion route' in order for the LEA to make a place available for him. The school is faced with using permanent exclusion as, in their own words, *'a strategy of support'*!

The work with the Social Services is another important link in welfare provision. One of the difficulties for School B is the fact that the boundaries of social work teams are often not co-terminous with those of the school and it is difficult for schools to deal with different teams of social workers. This adds to the problems caused by students who come from outside the catchment area (one-sixth of School B's intake) whom one would expect to be under the jurisdiction of a different social work team. The school has successfully pressed for a designated officer at a senior level to be the school's liaison person. Another difficulty has been the lack of information that has been given to the school. The school stresses the need to be given feedback on referrals since, apart from the time and effort that goes into a report, schools need feedback to inform their practice as well as to keep their records up to date. Youth Justice Teams, for example, regard information on matters such as cautions as private and not the concern of the school.

Links with the police are valued by both schools. In School A, they describe the relationship as 'brilliant' and recognize the role they can play in improving pupil behaviour. A youth action group was established with the help of the local community constable and events have been organized for senior citizens. In School B, the police came into school as part of the PSE programme for each year and they have had prisoners from the local prison (including 'lifers') come and speak to the pupils. There are also good links at strategic level with regular meetings between heads in the city and the police chiefs.

INTER-AGENCY CO-OPERATION AND CO-ORDINATION

So far in this chapter, the focus has been on links between outside agencies and schools. This, however, does not address the need to have co-ordination across the different agencies. In this section, we look at how School B has addressed these issues in innovative ways with considerable success.

School B and its pyramid have sought to involve as many agencies as possible and at the highest possible level. Pyramid heads meet on a monthly basis and try to spend some time during each meeting addressing common issues. They have invited agencies to give a presentation and have looked at issues such as child protection, occupational therapy, the EWO service, etc. In each case, practice has improved as a result of shared understanding and negotiation of roles. The organization of the pyramid is described as being 'professional' (minuted meetings, own secretariat and headed notepaper) and this is said to encourage other agencies to send their executive officers to the meetings. The group of pyramid heads has been on fact-finding visits to Holland (to look at pastoral care with specific reference to drugs) and to Scotland (to look at inter-agency work there).

EWOs meet the governors once a term and there are well attended meetings between heads and agencies involved with social welfare (Educational Psychologists, social workers and welfare officers). The meetings were set up to reduce problems of inter-agency working. Each meeting has a different focus and an input by a member of the group. This is again followed by discussion.

An even more original development is the establishment of a Governors' Welfare Committee. This committee grew out of the governors' interest and involvement in pastoral matters. Termly meetings between governors and pastoral staff were extended so that the former could take a more active part in the pastoral welfare of pupils. To enable this to happen, the subcommittee was doubled in size in order to cope with the increased workload. The local community was 'trawled' to co-opt suitable members such as local vicars, community policemen, psychologists and probation officers. Members of the group agree to join a school year group and follow it through the school. They meet with pastoral heads and parents to discuss problems. They have found that parents with children in difficulty often react more positively to other parents and laymen than they do to professionals. In order to keep up to date on a range of issues, the committee has introduced 'welfare teas' to which all governors and teachers are invited. Relevant professionals are invited to talk about issues of concern such as youth justice, child prostitution, one-parent families, the Children Act, etc.

ISSUES ARISING

The most striking and recurrent theme is that of overload. Each professional can give clear examples of this: the Educational Psychologist who only has half a day a fortnight to spend in each medium to large secondary school; the SENCO in School A with virtually half the school requiring SEN assistance and the nursing sister with a caseload of 2000 children. In order to survive, they have, as the Senior Registrar linked to School A puts it, 'to create obstacles to make them (pupils/parents) go through'. All the agencies have to filter cases so that only the most serious and/or urgent are dealt with. The Pupil Referral Service (PRS) linked to School A deals with requests for places in referral units centrally; schools draw up a list of those to be seen by the Educational Psychologist; social workers have a restricted caseload based on priority cases. This 'triage' is driven by the availability of resources and often not governed by the needs of the individuals. Professionals are inevitably compromised in their judgements by their knowledge of resource limitations and by their contractual obligations to their employers.

The Warnock Report, when quoting the figure of 20 per cent of pupils requiring special needs support, could not possibly have anticipated the uneven geographical distribution exacerbated by 'open enrolment', 'opting out' and the continued existence of grammar schools (or schools exercising selection that are grammar schools in all but name). One hidden danger is that pupils only receive attention when their needs are greatest and that once there has been some improvement, the help is often withdrawn. An extreme example of this is the case of a mother of a Y9 pupil in School A who was asked to come to school because of concerns about her son's behaviour. The mother happened to mention that at one time the boy had had a statement. The school looked into it and discovered that she was, in fact, correct. He had been given a statement in the primary school and had made considerable progress at the time. His statement had subsequently been removed with the result that there had been no consolidation of his progress and his behaviour had deteriorated because of problems he encountered with his work.

Not only are the cases filtered but the professionals have to prioritize tasks and may be unable to carry out the most effective, and arguably most useful, aspects of their job. For example, the school nurse in School A is unable to work with families on a long-term basis or train staff in schools. Solity and Bickler (1994, p. 25) refer to Kohli and Dare's chapters in their book. Both suggest that 'one of the consequences of resource problems is that professional groups retreat into narrow definitions of their territory, or even, as is the case with social work, to the statutory minimum'. At the same time, this intensification of workload is accompanied by enhanced expectations and a greater degree of accountability and media scrutiny and any shortcomings are harshly treated by the public. The stress and illness that result are referred to frequently by the head and deputy of School B.

The issue of workload is, of course, inextricably linked to resources. A number of examples have emerged which show that funding is inadequate. Too little time is spent in school and the services are stretched. The dilemma for the LEA is to decide to what extent they should retain central control of resources and to what extent they should run down central services allowing schools to determine their own needs and purchase help as required. The dangers of the latter strategy appear to be that, first of all, money that goes into school for one purpose can all too easily be diverted and, secondly, if the services are run down beyond a certain level, the system is unable to cope with any extreme cases which require the support of outside agencies.

Changes in legislation and the tightening up of procedures have been predictably accompanied by burgeoning bureaucracy. With insufficient clerical assistance, too much time is being spent by the professionals in filling in forms. The conflict arises when, in the absence of accurate records, it is difficult to provide for the child's needs across different agencies. The SENCO in School A should technically have over 500 IEPs as specified in the 1993 Education Act. She refuses, however, to 'bludgeon colleagues into coming up with things that are not improving things in the classroom and outside the classroom'. She feels that 'to be worthwhile, these must result in raising achievement and self-esteem for staff and pupils'. Instead, she is trying to work 'in the spirit' rather than to the letter of the law knowing full well that OFSTED (DfEE, 1995) will be looking in the future at how well schools are catering for the needs of special needs pupils.

One of the keys to successful inter-agency co-operation is communication. In the literature (Webb, 1989; McLaughlin, 1989) there is a long list of obstacles to successful communication, some directly related to resources: time, accessibility, intensification of work, and others related to differences of perspective: narrow professional perspectives, unequal status, ignorance of methods of working, territorial problems, professional jealousies, stereotyping. It follows that the more contact and more opportunities to compare practice and reflect on the processes at work, the better the understanding, mutual trust and co-operation is likely to be. The quality of communication is strongly influenced by personal factors and this is bound to cause unevenness in the system. In School A, joint meetings have proved successful but are not as regular as they would have wished and, therefore, personal contacts are less common. In School B, they lament the frequent staff changes in some agencies but have systems in place which do promote regular meetings and mitigate some of the problems. Solity and Bickler recognize the weaknesses: 'whilst it is admirable to encourage and legislate for collaborative working between different services, it is notoriously difficult to achieve in reality'. They quote (1994, p. 15) the Department of Health's (1990, p. 31) review of English local authorities' child care statements:

simply asserting the need for co-operation does not of course produce it (although it may well be a necessary stage in achieving it), and research inspections have repeatedly indicated that 'departmentalism' at the local level is a persistent obstacle to effective working with children and families.

Training, too, emerges as an important issue. All schools, for example, should have training in child protection issues. Student teachers, ill-prepared for their pastoral role (cf. Calvert and Henderson, 1995), have often received no specific training on child protection issues. In School B they are confident that all staff are aware of child protection issues and the need for refresher courses every few years. Teachers have legal responsibilities and a failure to observe the correct procedures can have serious consequences. For example, in cases of abuse, staff must not ask leading questions; they must report all allegations to the Child Protection Liaison Teacher and they cannot promise to keep disclosures secret.

The issue of disclosures is also very important when information about sexual activity is given by a pupil. If a teacher believes that a girl has behaved unlawfully by having underage sex, she must be counselled to inform her parents. If the girl refuses, the teacher, providing there are no child protection issues (cf. DfE Circular 5/94), must inform the head and the parents are informed. However, if the child goes to the Youth Clinic and has a positive pregnancy test, she can be counselled about an abortion and this can be carried out *without the knowledge of the parents*. While not advocating the latter route, there could be circumstances where one might argue it to be in the child's best interests.

Finally, there is often a reluctance, particularly in the case of abuse or neglect, to 'start the ball rolling', given the risks and the effort involved. As the Educational Psychologist for School A said, 'someone has to decide to make the case multi-disciplinary'. She feels she has both the 'clout' and the confidence to take action. Others might feel less confident and schools often fear involving the social services, for example, in case a child is put into care. Schools also fear damaging relationships with parents and forget that the needs of the 'client', that is to say the child, are paramount in the Children Act 1989. In the case of actual injury, there must be no delay as 'injury constitutes objective evidence' (Adams, 1995, p. 175). In stronger terms, Adams (ibid., p. 173) states, 'the school is a child protection agency' and teachers 'cannot risk inaction where they have a concern or suspicion of abuse'.

POSSIBLE RESPONSES

Before looking at specific responses, it is probably worth airing briefly an objection against teachers and other professionals making even more efforts concerning the welfare of the child. Some, like Turner (1996), argue that, given the levels of teacher stress in school and the burgeoning workload, teachers should not 'get drawn into areas of a pupil's welfare which they have little or no control over and have minimal effect upon'. Turner believes that 'the school does not have the time, expertise or resources to resolve conflicts within a family so should not get involved directly'. He supports one of the main points made repeatedly in this book that 'pastoral care is the care of learning' (and) 'it must be firmly rooted in the learning situation'. However, as has been pointed out by Klein (1996, p. 1), 'schools are uniquely placed among all agencies to be able to identify children who are being neglected. No other service sees children as frequently, at such close quarters and in as wide a range of activities.' It follows, therefore, that teachers have a role to take appropriate action and have a duty to do so.

Given the complexity of inter-agency collaboration and the sometimes insurmountable problems that schools and other agencies face, how can schools be more successful in involving others? The extent to which the school uses other agencies will depend on a variety of factors: the philosophy of the school and LEA; the level of need; local factors such as the accessibility and location of the different agencies and economic factors inside and outside the school.

These measures may indeed invite criticism in that they will almost inevitably involve more work and a greater call on resources. Nevertheless, some might be considered appropriate and feasible. To borrow a phrase, 'with sophistication comes complexity' (Stoll and Spink, 1996, p. 26) and, without doubt, more sophisticated responses to children's needs are available, but at a cost.

First of all, schools need to review their provision thoroughly. It is probable that creeping incrementalism has arisen from new legislation and responsibilities. They must decide what measures to take on the basis of value and feasibility. They need a clear vision of what they want to achieve. The head of School B asserted 'We've pushed the inter-agency work because we believe in it'. They have, over a period of years, continued to take stock and have arrived at a position where 'the system is good, the system is in place but we would like increased resources to make it work more effectively'.

They must focus on three key elements identified by Craft (1980): an internal co-ordinator, a team within the school and clear channels out of school to neighbourhood welfare services. To maximize the contribution of the internal co-ordinator(s), attention should be drawn to the secretarial, administrative and technical support they need to carry out their tasks effectively. As Downes (Chapter 6) argues, many tasks can be done more cost-effectively in schools by non-teachers. Teams of teachers might be required to meet the needs of SEN pupils, to deliver PSE and/or careers, to tutor pupils and to establish home–school links. Clear channels can be provided by organizing regular meetings which involve a range of agencies. These can not only help to increase and strengthen the links but also help to create common perspectives in organizations that all too often have very different agendas (Klein, 1996). Inter-agency training can support this. School B's use of pyramid liaison and the Governors' Welfare Committee stand out as useful models of ways of increasing involvement, sharing problems, clarifying roles and learning and reflecting together. School B has also sought actively to establish links at both a strategic (e.g. Police Commander) and operational level (community policeman) and to have a single named individual in each agency with whom to work.

They are also examples of ways of using the support services in an advisory capacity rather than involve them exclusively in direct intervention. This can enable teachers to be more effective and can help prevent problems. In the case of particular behavioural difficulties, School A has enlisted the help of referral staff and special schools to advise staff rather than wait for an exclusion. Similarly, as Normington and Kyriacou (1994) report, case conferences are 'more effective' and 'positive in tone' before exclusions rather than after.

Our study suggests that, although the case study school welcomed the contribution of outside agencies, there are still barriers between the school and outside. Evidence suggests that other professionals would like to play a fuller role in the work of the school and would welcome even more involvement. Evidence from elsewhere refers to some schools being regarded as 'no-go' areas for social workers and probation officers. The conclusion one could draw is that schools can, in some cases, be over-defensive and territorial in their dealings with outside agencies. The senior teacher at School A was prepared to concede that 'we need to look more creatively at what we are providing. Schools need to be more flexible and we need more of a shared ethos.' One overwhelming reason for involving other agencies inside schools is that not only do pupils bring problems to school, the school is often part of the problem! It may be worth considering the value of an on-site nurse/counsellor who can take a lead role and provide a bridge with the health services and others.

Finally, action plans must be specific and some process of monitoring and evaluation must take place. As McGuiness (1989, p. 142) puts it:

Educationalists are regularly exhorted to evaluate their progress, yet, for various reasons, little evaluatory activity occurs. There is almost a suggestion that the activity itself is valuable – that what teachers do is worthwhile, independent of the effects of what they do.

Stoll and Fink (1996, p. 166) put it another way: what gets assessed, gets valued and 'if schools do not measure what they value, what others choose to measure will be valued'.

CONCLUSION

This chapter set out to put the work of the schools and the different agencies in context. We have seen how changes in society and in education have increased the demands that are made on schools and, by extension, the agencies that they rely on. We have seen some of the problems involved in inter-agency collaboration. Normington and Kyri-acou (1994, p. 14), for example, state that 'various studies have indicated that effective collaboration and co-operation between agencies is difficult to achieve because of high case-loads, poor communication between agencies, and ill-defined role responsibilities that can easily lead to delays and misunderstandings'.

The case studies have presented two different schools and the ways in which they have tried to use the agencies to best effect. It might prove helpful at this stage to give a checklist of measures that schools can adopt or adapt:

- the redefining of clear policies and procedures (with lists of contact names and numbers available);
- a base in school for EWOs, nurses, etc.;
- an extension of the responsibilities of school nurses, etc.;
- regular inter-agency meetings;
- joint inter-agency briefings;
- increased involvement of governors and members of the local community;
- greater streamlining of lines of communication (link contacts);
- the use of clusters or pyramids to pool expertise and resources;
- service-level agreements rather than *ad hoc* arrangements.

As was stated earlier in the chapter, there is no suggestion that the case study schools are representative of the 5000 secondary schools in the UK. They were chosen because they highlight particular aspects of inter-agency provision: high demand for services, severely limited resources and a measure of initiative in harnessing the services that are available.

On the basis of the evidence, which arguably reflects the experience of many schools, especially those in urban or deprived areas, it is difficult not to arrive at the conclusion that the dedicated teachers, other professionals and, of course, the 'clients' (the pupils) are often being let down by the system.

Although provision might always be inadequate to meet the needs of pupils with such diverse and often severe problems, it is vital that we maximize the benefits of inter-agency working. A failure to do so could only lead to a worsening of the situation in some schools to the detriment of all those who work there.

REFERENCES

Adams, S. (1995) Child protection. In Best, R. *et al.* (eds) *Pastoral Care and Personal-Social Education.* London: Cassell.

Best, R., Lang, P., Lodge, C. and Watkins, C. (eds) (1995) *Pastoral Care and Personal-Social Education: Entitlement and Provision.* London: Cassell.

Calvert, M. and Henderson, J. (1994) Newly qualified teachers: do we prepare them for their pastoral role? *Pastoral Care in Education,* **12**(2) (June).

Calvert, M. and Henderson, J. (1995) Leading the team: managing pastoral care in a secondary setting. In Bell, J. and Harrison, B. T. (eds) *Vision and Values in Managing Education: Successful Leadership Principles and Practice.* London: David Fulton Publishers.

Cleveland (1988) *Report of Inquiry into Child Abuse in Cleveland* (Butler-Sloss Report). London: HMSO.

Craft, M. (1980) School welfare roles and networks. In Best, R. *et al.* (eds) *Perspectives on Pastoral Care.* London: Heinemann Educational.

Dare, J. (1994) Child psychiatry. In Solity, J. and Bickler, G. (eds) *Support Services: Issues for Education, Health and Social Service Professionals.* London: Cassell.

Department for Education (DfE) (1994) *Code of Practice on the Identification and Assessment of SEN.* London: HMSO.

Department for Education and Employment (DfEE) (1995) *Circular 10/95.* London: HMSO.

Department of Education and Science (DES) (1988a) *Working Together for the Protection of Children of Abuse: Procedures within the Education Service,* DES Circular 4/88. London: DES/WO.

Department of Education and Science (1988b) *The Education Reform Act.* London: HMSO.

Department of Health (1990) *Child Care Policy: Putting It in Writing.* London: HMSO.

Desforges, M. (1995) Separation, divorce and the school. In Best, R. *et al.* (eds) *Pastoral Care and Personal-Social Education.* London: Cassell.

Hodgson, K. and Whalley, G. (1992) The 1989 Children Act: some implications for pastoral care. *Pastoral Care in Education*, **10**(3), 20–1.

Home Office/Department of Health/DES/Welsh Office (1991) *Working Together – Under the Children Act, 1989*. London: HMSO.

Hutton, W. (1996) *The State We're In*. London: Vintage.

Klein, R. (1996) The pain and misery that go unheeded. *Times Educational Supplement*, 1 March.

Kohli, R. (1996) Social work. In Solity, J. and Bickler, G. (eds) *Support Services: Issues for Education, Health and Social Service Professionals*. London: Cassell.

McGuiness, J. (1989) *A Whole-School Approach to Pastoral Care*. London: Kogan Page.

McLaughlin, C. (1989) School management and disaffection. In Reid, K. (ed.) *Helping Troubled Pupils in Secondary Schools*, Volume 2. Oxford: Blackwell.

Maden, M. (1996) *Greenwich–TES Annual Education Lecture – 1996: Divided Cities: Dwellers in Different Zones, Inhabitants of Different Planets*. London: TES.

Normington, J. and Kyriacou, C. (1994) Exclusion from high schools and the work of the outside agencies involved. *Pastoral Care in Education*, **12**(4), 12–15.

OFSTED (1995) *Guidance on the Inspection of Secondary Schools*. London: HMSO.

Russell, P. (1992) Boundary issues: multidisciplinary working in new contexts – implications for educational psychology practices. In Wolfendale, S., Bryans, T., Fox, M., Labram, A. and Sigston, A. (eds) *The Profession and Practice of Educational Psychology*. London: Cassell.

Solity, J. and Bickler, G. (eds) (1994) *Support Services: Issues for Education, Health and Social Service Professionals*. London: Cassell.

Stoll, L. and Fink, D. (1996) *Changing Our Schools*. Buckingham: Open University Press.

Tomlinson, S. (1995) Home–school links. In Best, R. *et al.* (eds) *Pastoral Care and Personal-Social Education*. London: Cassell.

Turner, R. (1996) Stress in the secondary school: a management strategy for reducing stress among staff. *Pastoral Care in Education*, **14**(3), 3–5.

Webb, S. (1989) Interdisciplinary and inter-agency support. In Reid, K. (ed.) *Helping Troubled Pupils in Secondary Schools*, Volume 1. Oxford: Blackwell.

Whitney, B. (1994) *The Truth about Truancy*. London: Kogan Page.

CHAPTER 6

Resourcing pastoral support

Peter Downes

THE GROWING AWARENESS OF THE COST OF THE EXPANDING PASTORAL SYSTEM

Over the last decade the introduction of Local Management of Schools (LMS) has greatly increased our knowledge and understanding of the costing of education. Within schools, that new wisdom has been mainly applied to the costing of premises, 'capitation' (a familiar but now out-dated term referring to expenditure on resources – books, equipment and materials – directly used by pupils in the classroom) and to staffing costs (teaching and non-teaching). Relatively little work has been done at school level on sub-costing other aspects of the school's work. The purpose of this chapter is to explore in more detail how such a sub-costing could be applied to pastoral support and what positive benefits might be derived from it. At the same time, we have to be aware that, with increasingly tight budgets in schools, all expenditure has to be soundly justified and this should be applied to something as nebulous as 'pastoral support' just as much as to other more clearly measurable features of school life.

One could argue that pastoral care is more a reflection of the school's ethos than an aspect of school life which can be neatly pigeon-holed and quantified. I have a great deal of sympathy with this view. It is often the apparently casual interchange between a teacher and a pupil outside lessons, in the playground or even in the bus-queue that provides pastoral support or encouragement. Forty years ago, the head of a secondary school might have been able to assume that 'pastoral care' happened as a matter of normal routine between teacher and taught, with a particular expectation on the form tutor to deal with any indi-vidual problems which may have arisen. In the last twenty years, we have rightly come to see that pastoral support needs to be more struc-tured and we have put in place a variety of pastoral systems.

What LMS now enables us to do is to put a price label on that system and to consider whether or not the pupils are getting good value for money from the investment. This book makes it clear that the pastoral programme can be delivered in a number of ways. For the purposes of the calculations in this chapter, I am assuming that Personal and Social

Education (PSE) is treated as a timetabled subject and that its costs are built into the curriculum delivery part of the school's budget. Many schools now adopt the principle of disbursing curriculum-based funding according to a formula and this should apply to PSE as well. The details of the formulae vary from school to school but they are usually related to the number of periods taught by the department, weighted for the age of the pupil, roughly in line with the weighting of the Age Weighted Pupil Unit (AWPU) by which the school receives its funding. This recognizes that the materials needed for older pupils are usually more expensive than for younger.

I am also assuming that Careers Education and Guidance is provided as part of the curriculum cost although it is recognized that some of the work may well be done by tutors in 'pastoral time', for example, through interviews for Records of Achievement and Personal Learning Plans. Given those assumptions, the costs of the pastoral support system are:

(a) tutor time (registration, assembly, tutorial time);

(b) printing and materials costs associated with tutor time (e.g. photo-copying of worksheets, questionnaires);

(c) pastoral staff time (heads of year, heads of house, and any deputies they may have who are not also tutors);

(d) pastoral staff responsibility points;

(e) senior management team time (that proportion which is devoted to pastoral matters);

(f) administrative support to the pastoral and (a proportion of) senior management teams;

(g) equipment directly related to the pastoral work of the school, for example, enhanced telephone systems, computer links;

(h) outside agencies (e.g. educational welfare officers) although in most cases the costs of these are not delegated to schools but held centrally by the LEA.

Let us look at the major elements in this checklist in turn, attempting to cost our typical current practice and speculate on alternatives, remembering all the time that the aim is not to save money absolutely but rather to make the best use of the available time, in other words, to achieve the best value for money.

COSTING THE PASTORAL STRUCTURE

The school on which the costings in this chapter are based is a large 11–18 comprehensive school. There are 1850 pupils, including 350 in the Sixth Form. There are ten forms of entry and each year group contains about 290 pupils. The size of the school was an important factor in guiding the senior staff and governors towards the adoption of a relatively expensive model of pastoral support. The school is divided into three sections (Years 7/8 Lower School, Years 9/10/11 Middle School, Years 12/13, still called the Sixth Form), each with a deputy head as co-ordinator-in-chief. Throughout the school there is a system of four houses and in each section of the school there is a head of house. This model can be described as expensive because it involves twelve pastoral staff, all with non-contact time for dealing with pupil matters, and all holding responsibility points. The school has always felt that such an investment is essential in a large school spread over a large campus. Every pupil is attached to a form-group linked directly to a sectional house which has five to seven/eight groups in membership. The house perspective is reinforced by the physical layout of the school which gives each house a clearly designated area and thereby gives each pupil a defined environment (form-room, social area, toilets, locker, head of house office) with which to identify.

At the heart of the pastoral system is the form tutor. S/he is attached to a tutor group for 30 minutes per day for a tutor-group activity or assembly, plus a further 15 minutes for registration. With a group of 30 pupils s/he spends 3 hours 45 minutes (3.75 hours) in total, giving each pupil a notional 7.5 minutes of individual attention. The time used will be divided broadly into three: purely administrative tasks (taking the register, handling any official school matters, giving out notices, passing on messages); collective tutor-group activity; individual contact with pupils (talking over problems, following up day-book entries, helping with option choices and a thousand and one other important pastoral matters). Form tutors constantly complain that there is not enough time 'to get to know the pupils as individuals'. This gives a clear indication that we must try to find ways in which we can minimize unproductive time and maximize the valuable personal contact.

The average daily cost of a teacher, excluding heads and deputies and excluding responsibility points is, in 1996, £100 per day (except in the South East where extra salary is given for the cost-of-living weighting). Given that the maximum contact a teacher has with pupils during the working day is 5 hours 45 minutes, it can be seen that the teacher's time is 'worth' 30 pence a minute – an expensive commodity. For example, if in a six-form entry school, six tutors spend 20 minutes sitting in an assembly on three days a week, the school has spent £108 on that activity. If that pattern is repeated for all Year groups from 7 to 11, the cost per week is £540, amounting to £20,520 in a full school year (give or take a few exceptional weeks for work experience absence, mock and GCSE exams, etc.). What value has been obtained from that investment? The form tutors may have shared in the spiritual uplift of the assembly, have heard about what is going on in school (which they should have known already) and have enabled good order to be maintained. Is that a sufficient return on the price paid?

An alternative use of time might be for some or all of the form tutors to withdraw from assembly to give their valuable time to what they all consider the most important aspect of their work – individual contact with pupils. If two pupils were able to get ten minutes each of personal support during an assembly, three times a week totalling six pupils per week, the tutor group of 30 pupils could all have a one-to-one interview on a six-weekly cycle, *in addition* to any time given in registration or scheduled form tutor periods. The value to the school of such an intensive approach to personal support and intervention cannot easily be calculated. Early intervention with pupils with academic problems arising from lack of motivation, especially boys, will pay handsome dividends in terms of better GCSE results. This not only improves the school's overall academic status, it may well mean, in the case of schools with sixth forms, a higher staying-on rate. This increases the income to the school from having more pupils in the higher age ranges.

Let us move on to look at senior pastoral staff time, that is to say, the time we give those who are not form tutors, usually heads of year/house, plus any assistants they may have. Their time costs come in two parts: the registration/assembly time at the above rates amounts to £67.50 per week, plus any non-teaching periods allowed them in addition to their routine non-contact periods. It is best to calculate the cost of a teaching period in a school by starting with the total teaching salary costs, take out the head and deputies and the responsibility points and then divide the remainder by the number of teaching periods in a week. A school with a staff with an average age profile and a 25-period week will have a unit cost of £1100 for every timetabled period over the full year. The exact figure will depend on the age profile of the staff, of course, but it is the principle rather than the mathematical detail which matters. An 11 to 16 comprehensive school, with a pastoral system based on years, might typically give a head of year three non-teaching periods for their 'pastoral work' and one period to an assistant. This amounts to a financial investment of £22,000 for the time element of the pastoral system. An important question needs to be asked. Is the time during the working day, when pupils are in school, being used effectively for direct contact with pupils, or is it being used for team meetings which could take place outside school time and still within the statutory 1265 hours?

The pastoral system also costs money for the responsibility points given to the heads of year/house. The irregular steps in the pay spine make it difficult to generalize about the cost of a point since it all depends on where teachers are on the annual incremental part of the pay spine, but we might guess at £1200 per point. The cost to a school with five heads of year, each with three responsibility points and each assisted by a colleague with one responsibility point would be £18,000. It is difficult to say with certainty whether or not pupils get value for money from their pastoral system, but here are some of the questions that need to be asked: What is the time delay between a parental letter/request/complaint being received and action? How long does it take a head of year to follow up a disciplinary referral from within school? Do heads of year meet all the administrative deadlines within the school?

Exactly the same issues and costing can be applied to deputy heads who have a pastoral role, as most do. What proportion of their week is devoted to pastoral matters? How effectively is time used? Do they go over the same ground already covered by form tutors and heads of year? Are they doing in school time, that is to say when pupils are present, work which could be done just as effectively when pupils are not present? As a guide to over-worked heads and deputies, why not consider yourself to be doing a 37.5-hour week equated over a 46-week year (in the case of heads) and a 44-week year (in the case of deputies)? This gives a notional directed time of 1725 hours per year for a head and 1650 for a deputy. This amounts, for a deputy, to an extra two hours per day of the 190-day year, over and above all directed time commitments. The issue which needs to be focused on is the extent to which heads and deputies are carrying out their various tasks at the most appropriate time. If not, the school may not be getting best value for money.

MANAGING RESOURCES FOR PASTORAL CARE IN A TIME OF BUDGETARY PRESSURE

An analytical approach to the costing of pastoral care is the necessary first step to managing the limited resources available. In a sense, there are no resources ear-marked for pastoral care. The essence of LMS is that decisions about priorities must rest within the school, i.e. with the governors as advised by the head and staff. By breaking down the tasks and the costs as outlined above, the head is in a better position to give advice on whether or not the pastoral system is working effectively relative to the money spent on it.

The criteria for assessing the effectiveness of a pastoral system are highly debatable. Some might say that the only purpose of a pastoral system is to keep the pupils present in school, happy, on task, and committed, so that academic outcomes can be achieved, i.e. that there are no intrinsic and measurable objectives for a pastoral system outside academic performance indicators. Others might argue for different measures of success: school attendance figures, number of exclusions, proportion of the pupils in trouble with the police, the number of parental complaints about school, proportion of parents attending parental consultation evenings, pupil participation in extra-curricular activities, pupil participation in charity activities, extent of damage to property and graffiti, litter per square metre ... and so on.

Many schools do not yet quantify outcomes for the headings in the above list but perhaps the latest drive towards 'target-setting' might sharpen the thinking of senior management and governors. Even if they do, relating expenditure on pastoral care to outcomes is likely to be an imprecise art. A very large school might be able to pilot two parallel systems and see which one 'works better', always assuming that pastoral staff could agree on what 'working better' means.

In practice, changes will probably be at the margins, given the overall tightness in school budgets, and will focus on the issues outlined in the next three sections.

Making greater use of non-teaching staff to support the pastoral system

Schools which have carried out their internal time and motion studies of the work of senior staff have discovered that much of the time of a head, deputies, senior pastoral and departmental staff is spent on tasks which could be done more effectively and less expensively by non-teachers. In round figures, every hour of a basic teacher (not including responsibility points and senior management staff) can buy 2.5 hours (term-time only) of a non-teaching member of staff. Over the years since LMS has been established, the importance of this has only slowly penetrated the consciousness of the teaching profession. Many teachers still continue to spend their time doing routine administrative and clerical chores which could be done less expensively and probably more effectively by non-teaching staff. The poor value for money of teachers doing inappropriate work becomes even more marked when it is the more highly paid who are doing the low level tasks. Every school, and every part of every school, needs to be thinking seriously about what can be taken from the teachers and re-directed to non-teaching staff. Many forward-looking schools have done some or all of the following:

- appointed a dedicated exams officer to handle all external exam entries;
- appointed a non-teacher to run the daily absence cover rota;
- appointed technicians and/or administrative staff to assist with departmental or faculty administration;
- appointed secretaries to give direct personal day-by-day back-up to pastoral staff (taking messages, acknowledging telephone calls, sorting papers for action, filing pupil information);
- asked administrative staff to minute meetings, which has the double value of saving expensive time in writing minutes which then have to be retyped and also of keeping the secretary better informed so that s/he can deal with routine matters without having to disturb the senior staff.

At first, senior staff, both those with academic and those with pastoral responsibilities, may be reluctant to concede that others might be able to do tasks just as efficiently as they have been doing for years. Gradually, they come to realize that this is a better use of valuable resources. The last few years have seen a higher proportion of non-teaching staff and this is a trend which I expect to see accelerate in the coming years.

We need to remind ourselves of the aim of all these suggestions: it is to enable teachers and all those operating within the pastoral system to have the maximum time for working with pupils.

The role of improved technology

The development of technology can also come to the aid of pastoral staff at all levels, provided they are willing to let it do so. A number of more sophisticated ways are now available for taking registration: swipe cards, optical mark readers, radio-based registration systems. The networking of key offices, with immediate access to pupil data, can save a great deal of time. The availability of PCs or lap-tops means that pastoral staff with word-processing skills can enter data directly into the system, or can put work on to disk which can then be printed out by a secretary, thus saving time which can be fed back into supporting the pastoral staff. Data banks of computerized report statements are being developed and, after initial reservations have been overcome, are being seen as a way of improving the quality of reporting, saving pastoral staff and teacher time. As each year passes, telephone systems become ever more sophisticated and some schools have now put in place systems which direct external calls straight to the appropriate extension (thus saving a log-jam at the switchboard). These systems also allow calls to be saved, allowing parents wishing to contact pastoral staff during the day to leave a message at any time. This reduces the frustration felt by parents at being told by the switchboard operator, as they frequently are, that Mr X is not available and should be rung back later. Messages left in mail boxes tend to be shorter and leave the head of year/house free to ring back at a time more convenient to him or herself. These more sophisticated telephone systems may cost up to £5000 but, when the cost is spread over a number of years, save far more in terms of staff time and improve customer service. Improving the quality of service to parents is an important factor in parental choice of schools and so it might be that an investment in good communications may be a significant factor in increasing income to the school by attracting more pupils.

Awareness, training and greater flexibility

All these technological and administrative developments need to be costed, preferably with the same rigour suggested in relation to the use of staff time. In many cases, there will be an up-front capital cost but instead of seeing this as coming out of one year's budget (which it may have to do in terms of payment), it should be seen as an investment whose cost is spread over several years. There will also need to be training for those staff who have not yet developed the personal skills which will be needed to handle the technology and this will have a cost, albeit relatively small. The process of adopting new technology may seem daunting at first but the skills can be learned. After all, we profess to be promoting learning and flexibility in our pupils, so why are so many of us reluctant to learn new skills and show flexibility in our own routines? The reason is too often that learning IT skills and introducing greater involvement of non-teaching staff are seen as 'extras' crowding in to an already overloaded and pressurized existence. With persistence in the initial stages, they will soon come to be seen as real benefits to the process by releasing teachers and pastoral staff to concentrate on what they do best: helping children learn effectively and be happy and fully integrated individuals within the school.

Avoiding loss of income

Keeping pupils within the school has received greater prominence in the light of recent changes to LMS schemes whereby pupils excluded from a school during the academic year take away with them the remaining proportion of their Age Weighted Pupil Unit. This means that all reasonable efforts have to be made to find strategies to keep pupils within the school environment. The main reason is obviously the good of the individual pupils but an additional factor is the avoidance of loss of income mid-year where there are virtually no compensating savings to be made. A loss of, say, three pupils from a year group in October could cost the school 50 per cent of a £2000 AWPU times three: £3000. No savings could be made by reducing teaching costs mid-year, so the departure of these three pupils is a cash loss to the school. This is not an argument for never permanently excluding a pupil; there may well be circumstances where this is a necessary measure, as much for the long-term good of the offending individual as for the disrupted academic progress of the rest of the class. Costing the impact of 'trigger happiness' may nevertheless help to sharpen schools' thinking, especially when these losses are set against the pastoral investment costs outlined above.

LEA BUDGET GENERATION FOR PASTORAL CARE

New approaches to the way LEAs generate their school budgets are being pioneered. These 'activity-based' or 'needs-led' models break down the entire schooling process, including curricular and pastoral, into subheadings which are 'timed'. These subheadings, which may run to over 30 or 40 in the more sophisticated cases, are then globalized to produce the number of teachers required to provide a given level of service. The case for having a similar approach to the construction of the national budget for education has been made in *A Better Cake* (West *et al.*, 1994).

The earliest version of these models, starting from what heads saw as desirable, not surprisingly produced a need for more teachers. In reducing the number of teachers to what the LEA budget could afford, elected members could see how these reductions would impact on the quality of service provided. It has to be conceded that the main driver for such formulae is class size but the exercise of costing out the component parts of the life of a school is a valuable one in making people realize that precious resources are sometimes spent ineffectively.

CONCLUSION

I suggested at the beginning of this chapter that the head of 40 years ago might have managed a school without a complex pastoral structure, relying on the form tutor to sort out any problem which may arise. In the last 40 years, changes in society have put greater pressure on schools, creating more problems as well as raising expectations among parents. Many of the implications of these changes have been alluded to in the Introduction. The purpose of this chapter has been to focus attention on the financial factor in the pastoral systems which have necessarily developed over recent years. Lest this seemingly hard-headed approach to costing staff time may appear to jar with the spirit of the rest of the book, let me reaffirm my belief in the importance of pastoral support as a means, not merely of keeping children happy and out of trouble, but as a way of raising self-esteem and thereby improving academic performance.

This chapter has not set out to propose detailed solutions but to provoke a re-examination of the ways in which we provide pastoral support to children, seeking above all else to achieve quality and to give the best possible value for money.

REFERENCE

West, A., West, R. and Pennell, H. (1994) *A Better Cake: Towards a Rational Approach for Financing Education.* Leicester: Secondary Heads Association.

CHAPTER 7

OFSTED inspections: implications for evaluation and management

Brian Wilcox and Anne Taylor

INTRODUCTION

The four-year cycle of OFSTED inspections[1] has resulted in an annual production of several thousand commentaries on individual schools. These commentaries, or inspection reports as they are normally known, are organized under an invariant set of general headings as specified in the Inspection Handbook. Although the Handbook is available in separate versions for primary, secondary and special schools (OFSTED, 1995a, 1995b, 1995c), all three have the same basic structure of headings and subheadings which can be summarized as follows:

Educational standards achieved
attainment and progress
attitudes, behaviour and personal development
attendance;

Quality of education provided
teaching
curriculum and assessment
pupils' spiritual, moral, social and cultural development
support, guidance and pupils' welfare
partnership with parents and the community;

Management and efficiency of the school
leadership and management
staffing, accommodation and learning resources
efficiency of the school;

Curriculum areas and subjects
English, mathematics and science
other subjects or courses.

Inspection reports can be regarded therefore as constituting an archive of standardized descriptions of specific aspects of schools. These aspects essentially reflect an input–output model of schools. Outputs or outcomes are listed under the heading *educational standards achieved*. Inputs or factors contributing to these outcomes are represented by the remaining headings in the list.

This chapter is concerned with two basic questions:

What is the nature and status of OFSTED inspection reports and particularly of those sections which relate to pastoral care?
What significance do OFSTED inspections and reports have for those concerned with the practice and management of pastoral care?

In tackling these questions we shall be referring to pastoral care as it occurs in secondary schools. But first it is necessary to give the reader an indication of how pastoral care is treated in an OFSTED report.

FINDING PASTORAL CARE IN OFSTED INSPECTIONS

Although pastoral care is not one of the organizing headings of the Handbook much of what is understood by the term will be subsumed under the heading *support, guidance and pupils' welfare.* A secondary school inspection report typically has three or four paragraphs, perhaps three-quarters of a page, devoted to this heading. The text beneath it will be a highly condensed summary of judgements based on the extent to which the school:

provides effective support and advice for all its pupils, informed by monitoring of their academic progress, personal development and attendance;

has effective measures to promote discipline and good behaviour and eliminate oppressive behaviour including all forms of harassment and bullying;

has effective child care procedures;

is successful in promoting the health, safety and general well-being of its pupils. (OFSTED, 1995b, p. 54)

An example of the application of the first of these four criteria is given in the following extract from the inspection report of Urbley school.[2]

The school has chosen to invest considerable responsibility for pupil support and guidance in the personal tutors and to this end nearly all staff are involved, thus reducing group sizes. Under the overall leadership of the guidance management team, personal tutors are encouraged to monitor individual pupil development and pupils are encouraged to reflect on their progress and set themselves achievable targets. Whilst this approach assists pupils through demonstrating concern for their progress, it currently lacks a sharp focus on specific learning achievements and areas for improvement. The senior management team have plans to extend data gathering and monitoring of pupil progress in relation to academic progress.

From this account readers will understand how the school organizes pupil support and guidance (through a large number of personal tutors), what advantages (small tutorial groups) and disadvantages (lack of a sharp focus on progress in learning) have resulted from that and what the school envisages doing to improve the situation (developing the monitoring of academic progress).

Another aspect related to the first criterion – that of monitoring pupil attendance – is addressed in a later paragraph:

The school is aware that full attendance for all pupils is a key element in raising levels of achievement. To this end they have invested in a computerised attendance registration and monitoring system and are producing efficient feedback to tutors on pupil absence . . . . Progress on levels of absence has been made in recent years, but the school recognises that continued efforts need to be made to improve further.

Further paragraphs in this section of the report deal with the remaining criteria concerned with discipline and behaviour, child protection, and health and safety; on all of which the school is commended.

Readers will not, however, find all they may want to know about pastoral care in this one section of the Urbley report. They will need to examine some others. For example, under the section on *pupils' spiritual, moral, social and cultural development* we find a reference to the school having 'a clear set of values which are reflected in the orderly and purposeful conduct of school life'.

The section on *teaching* highlights a problem often associated with the use of the tutor period for teaching the pastoral curriculum:

The quality of the teaching of the guidance programme, which takes place during personal tutor time is inconsistent, . . . [and] generally poorer than the teaching of the National Curriculum and religious education. Some of the tutors use the guidance programme skilfully and the quality of teaching and progress of the pupils is good. Many of the lessons, however, are poorly prepared and structured, and the pupils make less progress. There is a need for the programme to be more closely monitored to ensure consistency across the whole school.

This issue of the use of tutor time is picked up again under *pupils' spiritual, moral, social and cultural development* in the suggestion that the guidance programme should also include 'an "entitlement" contribution to moral and social education for all pupils' in order to 'ensure greater consistency of content and delivery and . . . take account of the actual contribution of other subjects'.

The section also reports that another use of the tutor period is for pastoral assemblies while noting that few staff wish to hold an act of worship as part of tutor time. As a consequence 'the quality of collective worship is directly affected by limited opportunity'.

Although not mentioned in the Urbley report, comments on the provision of in-service education for tutors may sometimes be found under *staffing*.

Partnership with parents and the community and *leadership and management* are two further sections which may offer relevant insights into the quality of aspects of pastoral care. For example, under the former heading the Urbley report notes that:

Parents consider that they are well informed about their children's progress and reports are clear and helpful . . . . Parents of pupils with special educational needs are appropriately involved in the review of their children's progress.[3]

The practice of pastoral care requires endorsement by those with overall responsibility for school-wide leadership and management. This would seem to be the case at Urbley school:

Both the statement of school aims and the staff handbook emphasise the importance of creating a supportive and secure environment for pupils so they might develop as individuals and this intention is borne out in practice.

All of the above extracts from the Urbley report are examples of inputs to the system and their effects may be discernible in comments made on outcomes. For example, under *attitudes, behaviour and personal develop-ment* there are statements reporting the absence of bullying and the effectiveness of disciplinary procedures and the important role played by the student council in developing responsibility and involvement.

Also the outcome section on *attendance* adds further detail to what is said elsewhere on this topic by pinpointing the extent of unauthorized absence, particularly in Years 10 and 11.

Enough has probably now been shown to make the point that com-ments relevant to pastoral care will typically be found under several report headings. In this respect pastoral care is different from the more familiar subject areas such as English, mathematics, history, etc. – all of which are separately assigned their own specific section in an inspection report. These sections are also worth scrutinizing since all curriculum subjects potentially contribute to the pastoral care of pupils. The dis-persed nature of comments on pastoral care is of course consistent with the current 'breadth of the concept and the diversity and pervasiveness of the term's referents throughout the school' (Best, 1995, p. 5).

NATURE AND STATUS OF INSPECTION REPORTS

An inspection report as a whole may be regarded as a particular genre of school case study (Wilcox, 1992, pp. 45–7); one moreover which has the advantage of being available in the public domain.[4] The specific sections of reports may in turn be regarded as mini case studies. For example, the dispersed comments in a report relevant to pastoral care effectively provide an evaluative case study of that aspect of provision in the school concerned.

The availability of school inspection reports has opened up the pos-sibility of making comparisons of different aspects of provision *across* schools. Although OFSTED has already published a number of sum-maries based on inspection reports, as have also a few researchers (for respective examples see OFSTED, 1996 and Ouston *et al.*, 1996), we know of no analysis having yet been done on pastoral care. No doubt it is only a matter of time.

A crucial question about inspection reports and any use which might be made of them is whether they are trustworthy – whether, in the conventional language of evaluation, they are reliable and valid. The authors of the Handbook have attempted to meet these requirements by setting out what are implicitly assumed to be incontestable procedures and detailing how they are to be followed. At the heart of these is the notion that judgements are made by applying criteria. As we have already seen, the criteria employed are typically very general statements.

As a result they will be open to different interpretations. This is well understood by inspectors who, in practice, break down the criteria into more manageable sub-criteria or 'prompts'.

We then have to ask how are the sub-criteria to be applied? Perhaps by generating a further set of sub-criteria? But the same question can be asked again. We seem to be faced, then, with an infinite hierarchy of criteria. Since judgements *are* in fact made, we must assume that there is in the process of making a judgement, a kind of activity which is not itself criteria-governed. The basis for making a judgement can therefore never be completely pre-specified (Gilroy and Wilcox, 1997).

Why then should the judgements of inspectors be accepted as trust-worthy? This is too large a topic to pursue in detail here. (For a more adequate treatment see Wilcox and Gray, 1996, pp. 65–80 and 121–4.) However, we can say in brief that ultimately the trustworthiness of inspectorial judgements rests upon the extent to which they are corporately agreed:

The registered inspector[5] should ensure that the overall judgements about the school command the agreement of the inspection team. These corporate judgements can most easily be reached through discussion involving all team members towards the end of the inspection. Ultimately the registered inspector must adjudicate, if necessary, and have the final word on judgements to be included in his or her report. (OFSTED, 1995b, p. 33)

Several inspectors are likely to contribute judgements to an understanding of those aspects which relate to pastoral care (e.g. support, guidance and pupils' welfare). Their various judgements and insights will need to be reconciled into a form to which all can give their agreement. Pastoral care staff may take some comfort from the fact that judgements in their area are potentially corroborated by this kind of process. In contrast, judgements in most curriculum areas (mathematics, science, etc.) will in practice be made by a single specialist inspector.

Generating corporate judgements is not, however, a self-evident process and the Handbook gives no detailed guidance on how it should be carried out. The reader of an inspection report can never know exactly how, and how well, the process was conducted. Were the inspectors' judgements tested adequately in the crucible of debate? Do the time constraints of the inspection week allow rigorous scrutiny to take place? These are just two of the questions which might be raised.

Inspection, like other forms of educational evaluation, is never unassailable. Ultimately, an inspection has persuasive power rather than definitive validity. An inspection relies on the expectation that inspectors are trusted to make considered and just judgements. This requires, at the very least, the selection of those: who are competent in specific aspects of schooling; who have been, and continue to be, appropriately trained to inspect; and who work within a tradition of inspection which is capable of critiquing its own practice and developing it further. While OFSTED does have its trenchant critics (see Fitz-Gibbon, 1995), it may be said that as an *inspectorate* it has attempted to address these requirements more systematically and openly than any of its predecessors. Pastoral care staff should therefore regard OFSTED inspection reports as potentially valuable sources of insight into their area of work.

SIGNIFICANCE OF OFSTED INSPECTIONS FOR THE PRACTICE AND MANAGEMENT OF PASTORAL CARE

Despite the reservations noted above, OFSTED inspections do provide a means for the regular and systematic external evaluation of all major aspects of schools – evaluation which has no internal 'axe to grind'. Those concerned in a school with the practice and management of pastoral care should therefore regard an assessment of their area of responsibility by (it is to be hoped) impartial, expert colleagues from outside as an opportunity for further professional and organizational development. This potentially positive aspect of inspection is enshrined in the requirement that a school-wide action plan be implemented which takes account of any weaknesses identified. Even where pastoral care does not feature in any of a report's *key issues for action*, relevant sections may reveal, as we have shown in the example above, aspects where improvement is possible. Following an inspection, staff might therefore usefully draw up their own mini action plan or suitably modify their existing development plan to take account of comments made relevant to pastoral care. Conceived of in this way, OFSTED inspection becomes an integral, albeit occasional, element within the planning process.

The OFSTED Handbook is not only an inspection guide, it is also implicitly a set of descriptions of what is considered to constitute good practice for specific aspects of the school. The Handbook and its various sections provide a useful vocabulary of concepts and criteria which may help staff come to a better shared understanding of their professional concerns. Pastoral staff will understandably wish to familiarize themselves with the relevant parts of the Handbook in order to prepare for an inspection. Most teachers do want to be seen at their best during an inspection and to do so it is necessary to understand what the inspectors expect of them. Getting ready for inspection should not, however, become a cynical exercise of 'window dressing'. Preparation, if done intelligently and collectively, is likely to have a long-term and, it is to be hoped, beneficial effect on the thinking and practice of staff.

As already noted, comments related to pastoral care are dispersed throughout the Handbook in several sections. The task of familiarization is somewhat more difficult for pastoral staff than for their colleagues responsible for specific curricular subjects. Fortunately this problem has been addressed in a recent publication of the National Standing Committee of Advisers, Inspectors and Consultants of Personal and Social Education (NSCOPSE, 1996). This brings together all the relevant Handbook sections into a single document. In addition, the document considers each OFSTED section in turn and expands them into a set of more specific questions which, taken together, constitute indicators of good practice. For example, in the section on *leadership and management* good practice is characterized by schools which:

have a person who manages PSE across the curriculum;
have a clear line management structure for monitoring PSE;

include pastoral and PSE issues in the school development plan;
have a sex education policy, where appropriate, which meets statutory requirements;
ensure that the statutory elements of sex education within the science National
Curriculum are in place. (NSCOPSE, 1996, p. 16)

Although the document was designed to help schools prepare for
inspection and provide guidance for inspectors, it has a further and
arguably more important function as an instrument for self-evaluation.
Earlier attempts to introduce self-evaluation to schools in the late 1970s
and early 1980s were at best mixed and tended to represent pious
rhetoric rather than reality. Although, more recently, self-evaluation has
been recognized as an integral feature of school development planning, in
practice it is often neglected. Moreover, the self-evaluation of individual
aspects of a school's curricular provision remains relatively undeveloped.
Self-evaluation is even more of a challenge for school-wide aspects, such
as pastoral care, than for conventional subjects of the school curriculum.
The NSCOPSE document goes a good way towards meeting that challenge.

A further spin-off of OFSTED inspection has been the provision of
examples of innovative practice. Our recent experience of inspection and
evaluation indicates several strands of promising development in pastoral care. There is clearly renewed interest in tackling the traditional
academic–pastoral split. This is often associated with new structures
based on National Curriculum Key Stages and a more developed role for
form or personal tutors. Emphasis on the latter has pointed up the
necessity of good pupil information provided through an efficient IT
system. A school known to one of us is able to provide its tutors on a
weekly basis with an updated printout on pupils' academic and pastoral
progress.

Other promising developments which we have observed include the
involvement of senior management teams, and sometimes personnel from
local industry and commerce, in the mentoring of targeted groups of
pupils (e.g. those likely to be on the borderline of GSCE grades C/D).
Recent attention given to anti-bullying policies has led, in some cases, to
the use of 'peer counselling' of younger by older pupils. Such developments are leading to a rethinking of tutoring and pastoral skills generally. There are important implications here for both initial and
in-service teacher education, especially if all or most school staff are now
to be required to perform a tutor role.

Although the details given of such developments in inspection reports
are necessarily brief they may be sufficient for interested readers to
pursue further. Managers of pastoral care might therefore usefully look
at inspection reports of other schools, particularly those with similar
characteristics to their own. Inspectors will invariably have more
detailed knowledge of good practice than can be included in the small
number of paragraphs available to them in a report. Where inspectors
have other roles such as consultants, advisers or trainers there will be
opportunity to disseminate their greater knowledge more widely. The
experience of engaging in inspections has probably given many erstwhile

advisers a sounder and more up-to-date knowledge of what schools are doing in their field than was the case in the pre-OFSTED era. Pastoral staff, therefore, may well find that the experience of a specialist inspector or adviser is well worth tapping.

The OFSTED inspection system was conceived in the heat of political controversy and initially was strongly opposed by many teachers and educationists. Some five or so years on, a cooler assessment is possible. The value of regular inspection is now more generally recognized – certainly by politicians of all parties and by many senior staff in schools. Although reservations about methodology and procedures remain, there does seem to be a willingness that these should be tackled. Inspection is then set to remain an important part of the educational firmament. Pastoral staff can with confidence, therefore, regard OFSTED inspections and reports as offering not only a means of assessing their practice but also potentially a conceptual framework for its better understanding, an instrument for self-evaluation and a source of innovative development.

NOTES

1. OFSTED (Office for Standards in Education) is the non-ministerial body responsible for the inspection of schools by independent teams.
2. Urbley is a fictitious name given to the school to preserve its anonymity.
3. Governors, in their annual report to parents, are required to comment on progress made in providing for special educational needs.
4. OFSTED reports are also now available on the Internet. The address is http.//www.open.gov.uk/ofsted/ofsted.htm
5. The registered inspector is responsible for the inspection team and all matters relating to the inspection.

REFERENCES

Best, R. (1995) Concepts in pastoral care and PSE. In Best, R., Lang, P., Lodge, C. and Watkins, C. (eds) *Pastoral Care and Personal-Social Education: Entitlement and Provision*, pp. 3–17. London: Cassell.

Fitz-Gibbon, C. T. (1995) Ofsted, Schmofsted. In Brighouse, T. and Moon, R. (eds) *School Inspection*. London: Pitman.

Gilroy, P. and Wilcox, B. (1997) OFSTED, criteria and the nature of social understanding: a Wittgensteinian critique of the practice of educational judgement. *British Journal of Educational Studies*, **45**(1), 22–38.

NSCOPSE (1996) *A Guide to PSE and OFSTED Inspections*: National Standing Committee of Advisers, Inspectors and Consultants of Personal and Social Education. (Copies available from NSCOPSE, 59 Randall Road, Kenilworth, Warwickshire CV8 1JX.)

OFSTED (1995a) *Guidance on the Inspection of Primary Schools*. London: HMSO.

OFSTED (1995b) *Guidance on the Inspection of Secondary Schools*. London: HMSO.

OFSTED (1995c) *Guidance on the Inspection of Special Schools*. London: HMSO.

OFSTED (1996) *OFSTED Publications Catalogue: A Guide to OFSTED Publications 1993–95*. London: OFSTED.

Ouston, J., Fidler, B. and Earley, P. (eds) (1996) *OFSTED Inspection: The Early 'Experience'*. London: David Fulton.

Wilcox, B. (1992) *Time-Constrained Evaluation*. London: Routledge.

Wilcox, B. and Gray, J. (1996) *Inspecting Schools: Holding Schools to Account and Helping Schools to Improve*. Buckingham: Open University Press.

CHAPTER 8

Managing change in pastoral care: a strategic approach
Mike Calvert

INTRODUCTION

The last decade has seen an acceleration and intensification of change. Hargreaves (1994, p. 6) refers to 'a multiplicity of reforms and innovations' and 'rampant and remorseless change imposed from above'. The 'root and branch' changes (Hargreaves and Hopkins, 1991) affect every aspect of school life. The reforms are strongly criticized by Hargreaves and Goodson (1995) for their effect on the teaching profession:

Notwithstanding some real benefits for teachers in areas such as assessment expertise, the reforms have generally pandered to high-profile parents, diverted teachers' energies to public relations and paperwork, weighed teachers down with interminable testing requirements and overloads of content and caused a rush for early retirement. Teacher morale has collapsed at the same time as teacher stress has increased.

The results sound dramatic expressed in those terms but references to 'initiative fatigue' and 'innovation without change' are common.

This chapter begins by identifying what the special characteristics and circumstances of pastoral care might be. It goes on to present a model for change highlighting some of the challenges and potential pitfalls. The author is currently working with four case study schools who are undergoing changes to their pastoral systems. The schools are all state comprehensive schools of different sizes and age range. The schools were self-selecting in that they all expressed a wish to involve an external agent of change to support their change efforts. All the schools were focusing on the provision for PSE. The work is still ongoing but many lessons have already emerged from the study.

The chapter does not set out to provide guarantors of success but to identify factors which together will enhance the possibilities of bringing about successful change. The chapter will, at the same time, echo Fullan and Hargreaves' (1992, p. 4) warning that 'there are no quick fixes but there are quick failures'.

WHAT IS SPECIAL ABOUT PASTORAL CARE?

Managing change in the area of pastoral care is arguably different from that in other areas of school life for the following reasons:

- Pastoral care defies an unequivocal definition. As Best (1995) points out, 'twenty years of discussion, writing and theorizing have failed to achieve much more than a working consensus'. As we have seen in Bell and Maher's (1986) historical analysis no clear pattern of provision has emerged. These views are reinforced by Megahy (see Chapter 2). There can be said to be a lack of shared understanding and agreement as to the precise purposes and nature of pastoral provision and 'a lack of consensus as to the aims, nature, content, skills and processes of PSE work' (Calvert and Henderson, 1995, p. 71, referring to Shaw, 1994). An absence of a clear pedagogy for PSE and a discourse for discussing aspects of pastoral care puts this area at a clear disadvantage in relation to subject specialisms.

- It follows, therefore, that teachers who feel competent and confident in their own subject disciplines may, and often do, feel very different about their pastoral work. The lack of pre-service and in-service provision predictably results in a profession which feels ill-prepared for this aspect of its work. Schools appear to have directed the vast majority of their staff development efforts towards the National Curriculum since the late 1980s at the expense of non-National Curriculum areas such as pastoral care.

- Not only do staff feel less confident, they also have difficulty in identifying and articulating their needs. When interviewing teachers about their training needs, three things are immediately apparent:
  - the needs they identify are very disparate;
  - they find it difficult to locate where their needs lie or are unable or unwilling to identify them;
  - the reasons they give for a lack of satisfaction in the pastoral domain might mask other feelings or considerations.

- Because there are no National Curriculum requirements and there is a low level of understanding regarding appropriate methodology in PSE, for example, it is difficult for teachers to identify their own needs and for managers to both recognize their own and convince others of theirs.

- Pastoral care enjoys low status in many schools. Inferior status vis-à-vis the academic sphere, an overemphasis on academic results (Ketteringham, 1987) and the lack of support from management and government are just three manifestations. As a consequence, inadequate time, thought and resources are often allocated to it. Since teacher status is partly defined by the status attached to what they are doing in the eyes of others, it follows that in schools where pastoral care is perceived as low status, teachers may be less inclined to devote their efforts to it.

- Since pastoral care often lacks clear and precisely specified goals, there is little evaluation in this domain. That pastoral care is a whole school issue is not in dispute here, but have we, as practitioners or managers, the necessary sophistication to create, develop and monitor a system that can realistically be described as well integrated and coherent? And, if we do, how do we know? What performance indicators would provide the evidence of our relative success or failure in provision? We have seen in Chapter 7 how difficult it is for external evaluators to measure pastoral care. Internal monitoring is also beset with difficulties.

- Perhaps most important of all, is the very nature of pastoral care and the personal involvement that it requires. Because it concerns itself with relationships and human interaction it defies some of the more mechanical approaches that subject training often involves. It requires teachers to reflect on their attitudes and beliefs and calls for personal development that must be central to their role. Reflection is essential and can only be done over time. Quoting Fullan (1988, p. 197), Oldroyd and Hall (1991, p. 26) see the way of changing teachers' beliefs as being complex:

  Changes in beliefs are ... difficult to bring about: they challenge the core values held by a person regarding the fundamental purposes of education and they are often not explicit or recognised .... The relationship between behavioural change (e.g. teaching approach) and changes in beliefs is complicated ... [it] is reciprocal – trying new practices sometimes leads to questioning one's underlying beliefs; examining one's beliefs can lead to attempting new behaviour.

- Teachers need to reflect on the environment in which they work. Fullan and Hargreaves (1992, p. 13) describe this as the 'ecological perspective'. This environment is central to an appreciation of such key aspects of pastoral care as relationships, authority and learning. Such a global appreciation of the school is difficult for the busy teacher and might well prove overwhelming given the possibility of a number of contradictions and conflicts that might exist across different areas of school life. If, for example, pastoral care is dominated by concerns of discipline and control and the form tutor is seen in that light, it makes the task of fostering a caring, relaxed environment within the PSE classroom, where the individual's worth and contribution are valued, extremely difficult to achieve.

- A final issue is that of *déjà vu*. A number of teachers interviewed in the ongoing research can remember initiatives in the 1980s, a number of which were well funded and allowed for generous staff release and new materials. A number of these initiatives were not successful or their effects were eroded over time and some teachers have said that they fear 'another false dawn'.

Management of change in pastoral care is, therefore, management of an aspect of schooling which is more complex, less tangible, less clearly defined and which enjoys a lower status than that of the formal curriculum. It also has to cater for a mixed group of teachers with varying degrees of skill, knowledge and commitment who are overworked, stressed and reluctant to commit themselves further at a time of cutbacks in staff, budgetary stringency and negative judgements by politicians and organizations such as OFSTED. It is against this background that any change initiatives must be carried out.

DEVELOPING A MANAGEMENT OF CHANGE FRAMEWORK

The art of managing change is a complex one, made even more problematic in an educational environment where it is recognized that so little time is actually spent managing and planning. 'Development cycles' abound and they have become 'more complicated and multi-dimensional in an attempt to represent life more accurately' (O'Sullivan, 1995). In spite of its complexity, it is possible to break down the steps and consider them in turn. It is not the author's intention to produce an intricate working model, a 'tool kit' for managers in schools (Everard and Morris, 1996). Given the complexity of change situations, a 'best fit' approach which is responsive to context is recommended. Reassuringly, although the management of change literature is full of checklists, lists of questions and stages to be gone through, 'the similarities outweigh the differences' (Everard and Morris, ibid., p. 217) and as they state, it is possible to go round a golf course without using all the clubs!

Here are just three development models (Table 8.1), each offering a different degree of specificity. The Organization Development Model (ODM) focuses on the individual and the institution. It is defined by McCalman and Paton (1992, p. 120) as 'a process by which members of an organization can influence change and help the organization to state and achieve its goals better'. It focuses on three levels: individual motivation, group behaviour and organizational structure and management. (The ODM headings in Table 8.1 are taken from Warner Burke (1987) by McCalman and Paton.) At the heart of many ODM initiatives is the formation of teams within the workplace and the model reflects a move towards flatter management with greater autonomy and reliance on the internal resources of the organization (Mayon-White, 1993). The second model is the Person-Centred Action Model (PCA) which focuses primarily on teachers' developmental needs and concerns and emphasizes the individual (Marsh, 1994). The third is taken from *Skills for Life: Core Manual* (TACADE, 1994, pp. 21–3) and is specifically designed for senior managers and curriculum co-ordinators who have a responsibility for planning and managing change in the area of pastoral care. It offers schools:

the opportunity to identify the development needs of key agents for change concerned with young people's personal and social development within the school: the students themselves, their teachers, their schools as organisations and their families and communities.

Its philosophy is 'to place young people's personal and social development at the heart of the educational process' (p. 6).

For the purposes of this chapter and at the risk of over-simplifying the cycle, it might be helpful to look at the stages under the following headings:

- preparing for change
- planning
- acting and reflecting.

Table 8.1 Organizational development models

Organization Development Model	Person-Centred Action Model	TACADE Development Model
Phase 1: entry	Phase 1: establishing the project	Phase 1: prepare for change
• initial contact between organization and consultant;	• negotiating resources and support ('allies');	• establish a climate for change;
• clarification of roles.	• getting assistance from external consultants;	• recognize the need for change;
	• forming a team.	• develop the capacity to begin.
Phase 2: formalizing the contract	Phase 2: assessment and goal-setting	Phase 2: identify needs
• agreement of roles.	• data collection;	• acknowledge people's starting points;
	• feedback;	• identify the needs of students, teachers, school organization and the family/community.
	• goal-setting.	
Phase 3: information gathering and analysis	Phase 3: identifying a solution	Phase 3: evaluate provision
• data gathering;	• establishing criteria for solution;	• establish structures and strategies for evaluation;
• diagnosis.	• specific information provided for all possible solutions.	• identify and secure resources required.
Phase 4: feedback	Phase 4: preparing for implementation	Phase 4: consider the needs–provision gap
• summary of the data gathered;	• development of a game plan including:	• define the gaps between identified needs and existing provision.
• general discussion;	– developing supportive organization arrangements;	
• interpretation of what has taken place.	– training;	
	– providing consultation and reinforcement;	
	– monitoring and evaluation.	

Table 8.1 *Continued*

Organization Development Model	Person-Centred Action Model	TACADE Development Model
Phase 5: planning the change process • consultant generates ideas; • consultant acts as sounding board.	Phase 5: implementing the project • supportive strategies and training; • opportunities to reflect and plan.	Phase 5: specify a focus for change • prioritize specific area(s) for development informed by above.
Phase 6: implementing the changes • continuous involvement of consultant.	Phase 6: reviewing progress and problems • monitor success levels amongst teachers and later students.	Phase 6: identify intended outcomes • specify aims and objectives; • consider the implications of unintended outcomes as they arise.
Phase 7: assessment • what has gone before; • status quo; • what action steps are necessary in the future.	Phase 7: maintenance and institutionalization • plans to ensure continued support.	Phase 7: plan and take action • translate aims and objectives into specific time-limited targets; • secure the commitment of others; • identify key tasks and strategies; • define roles and responsibilities; • design monitoring and reviewing procedures.
		Phase 8: review • collect evidence of implementation; • identify barriers to implementation; • compare outcomes with intended targets; • consider the remaining and new gaps between needs and provision.
		Phase 9: re-enter the model • decide on appropriate re-entry point to continue the development process.

The grid (Table 8.1) suggests a rational sequence of actions that can be followed in order, but O'Sullivan (1995, p. 41) gives us the following warning: much of the time the nice logical structure of the cycle is an illusion, the reality being a more dynamic and unpredictable combination of forces which often feels messy and out of control. But he also reassures us that, in the hurly-burly of everyday life in a learning organization, that is quite normal.

Before leaving the detailed grid behind, it is worth highlighting the main recurrent features:

- the need to spend a great deal of time and effort on examining the status quo and on planning;
- the use of an external agent of change;
- the importance of teams;
- the adoption of a holistic approach to change.

What follows is a guide to the different stages and processes involved in the change process.

PREPARING FOR CHANGE

In this section we begin by analysing the situation and looking for ways of creating a climate for change.

Analysing the situation

Managing change is harder than some managers believe. Time is at a premium in school and the process can all too easily become hurried and partial. As a result, the diagnosis may be weak and the resistance too great for meaningful change to take place. In the first place, we need to ask:

- What is the presenting problem?
- Who is the problem owner (or minder)?
- What is the source or 'trigger' of the change (internal or external)?
- What is the nature of the change?
- What is its size and potential impact?

The following example from a case study school will serve to emphasize the importance of asking these questions and the need for clarifying aims and objectives at the outset.

School A   School A is an 11–14 comprehensive school with 450 pupils on roll. With only 18 staff, it is common for staff to have a number of responsibilities. At present there is no designated time for PSE. There is tutorial time in the morning but this is eroded by assemblies and form tutor administration. OFSTED, while praising the quality of pastoral relationships, criticized the PSE element, and resources have been set aside to help remedy this. A decision was taken to introduce a timetabled PSE lesson, taught by form tutors. The priorities for the school were to put together a programme for Y7–9 which would be manageable for, and acceptable to, staff. According to the deputy head 'the most important thing is to have a programme in place, costed, resourced and staffed'. A half-day meeting was held off-site with the deputy head, the heads of year and an external agent of change (the author). The deputy had intended the meeting to be about syllabus design but was encouraged to include management of change and the nature of pastoral care as important topics to be addressed. An open discussion was held and it emerged then, and at a subsequent staff meeting, that using form teachers would meet considerable resistance and staff would favour a volunteer rather than a conscript force.

From this example, the following observations can be made. The problem holder was the deputy head. He was approaching the 'problem' in a rational, pragmatic way. From the decisions that had already been taken, and from the views expressed in interviews, it is possible to summarize the school's standpoint at the outset:

- the school needed to change (because of OFSTED and staff dissatisfaction with the status quo);
- PSE can be taught by the form tutor (since he/she is the first pastoral contact);
- the staff are dedicated and experienced and will accept (and even welcome) change;
- heads of year are the best 'key players';
- the main issue is getting a programme together. The syllabus is defined by topics and 'with useful resources, the time to do it and the training' we can succeed;
- evaluation can be dealt with later;
- money is available for the release of staff, new resources and INSET;
- the agent of change will help with the INSET and syllabus design.

The impetus for change had largely come from the staff who were dissatisfied with the existing provision. However, in the early stages the decisions had been made by a senior member of staff who viewed the presenting problem in a different light to the key players. One very positive aspect of the meeting with the 'key players' was the deputy's willingness to shift ownership of the change to the team. The school, with such a small staff, is used to delegating responsibility and believes that the individual heads of year have the ability to carry out the changes. There is no suggestion of being 'left holding the baby' but of them being given the ownership and responsibility to carry out the task. Unfortunately, in this case, timetabling decisions are being taken late in the summer term. Since the staff who are to teach PSE are largely unconfirmed and the 'key players' not in place, this will inevitably hamper the necessary planning and training.

The importance of who the problem holder is, and how they perceive their situation, can be seen again in the brief example that follows.

School B School B is a small, rural comprehensive (11–18) school with 450 pupils on roll. The school wishes to move from an unsatisfactory situation in which form teachers teach PSE with different degrees of commitment and expertise to one in which staff with the necessary skills and commitment volunteer to teach. The head of PSE has recently been appointed head of lower school. Her workload is such that after two preliminary meetings with the author she has confessed that in the last six weeks 'I haven't had time to even think about PSE since you last came in' and has stated that it will be another six weeks or two months before we can meet again. She has been given the task of preparing a new syllabus ('I've been told to write a programme') and reveals her lack of confidence ('None of us have been trained'). She clings to the notion that 'once you've got the programme written, the rest of it may well fall into place'. In correspondence, she states that she thinks they will be 'muddling through for a while next term' (i.e. Autumn term).

In this example, the teacher was given the role of head of PSE and is technically the problem holder but is, in fact, simply the problem minder unable to cope with the demands of managing change. She feels overloaded and ill-equipped for the task, both in terms of managing the change, and in terms of curriculum design and pedagogy. Her role as 'gatekeeper' is preventing the agent of change from exercising any influence and, as a result, planned change is unlikely to take place.

CREATING THE CONDITIONS FOR CHANGE

Once one has identified what is to be changed and what the impact and extent of that change might be, the next step is to try to create the conditions for change. Carnall (1995, p. 6) sees commitment, involvement and shared perception as 'success guarantors' and identifies three necessary conditions for effective change:

- *awareness*: stakeholders (teachers in this context) understand and believe in the vision, the strategy and the implementation plans, etc.;
- *capability*: stakeholders involved believe they can develop the necessary skills and can therefore cope with and take advantage of these changes;
- *inclusion*: stakeholders involved feel that they value the new jobs, opportunities, etc. and *choose* to behave in the new ways (new attitudes, skills and ways of working).

The author stresses the word 'choose'. Research suggests that it is insufficient to show people what to do. As McLaughlin (1991) points out, new information in itself is insufficient and carries no guarantee that teachers will either apply or sustain it in action. Motivation is the key and beginning with teachers' needs is an important starting point. The rewards must outweigh the effort involved in changing or in Gleicher's (in Everard and Morris, 1996, p. 257) more sophisticated equation:

$C = f(ABD) > X$, where
C = change, which is a function (f) of
A = the extent of dissatisfaction with the status quo (present state),
B = clarity of vision of where we want to be (future state),
D = feasibility of the first practical steps for getting there and

X = the cost of the change, in both financial and psychological terms.

In most schools, staff commitment to pastoral care and change will vary tremendously. Everard and Morris (ibid.) recommend aiming for a small 'critical mass' who will bring about change.

Teamwork is seen as an essential part of organizational development (Peters and Waterman, 1982; Handy, 1985). There has been a marked shift away from rigid, hierarchical team models to flatter management and small, organic groupings. All too often, the hierarchical teams have not been successful for a variety of reasons. Take the following example:

School C   School C is an 11–18 school with 750 pupils on roll. Until four years ago the deputy head was the pastoral co-ordinator and 'loosely' oversaw the work of the heads of year. PSE was taught to Y10 and Y11 during a 70-minute lesson at the end of the afternoon. In the Lower School, it was delivered via tutor time and the work overseen by heads of year. The new head has been making changes including the creation of the post of head of PSE. The school is changing to delivering PSE via form tutors and sees the heads of year as central to overseeing the work of the year teams.

In this example, the use of heads of year as key players could represent a weakness. In the past they have not been successful in their support for PSE. The school has been encouraged to consider a different structure identifying a core team based on commitment and ability and not on hierarchy.

Ideally the teams can be made up of a mixture of staff whose membership is based on commitment and identified strengths. A newly qualified teacher with a good grounding in counselling might well form a useful member of a team of 'key players'. The inclusion of senior staff, especially if they occupy a lower-profile role (Stoll and Fink, 1996), adds status and perspective to the group. The teams need to be given (or negotiate for themselves) a role description. As Lodge (1995) makes clear, a job title is not sufficient. What is needed is a clear understanding of how the structure works and what the lines of communication are. Lodge (ibid., p. 32) goes on to say that 'such clarity helps to avoid misunderstandings about role, which have especially dogged pastoral team leaders'.

One benefit of having teams is the creation of support networks. As Rylance (Rylance and Evans, 1993a, 1993b) found, when bringing about change in pastoral care provision in a number of schools, small development teams of interested participants were instrumental in helping teachers devise strategies that they could use in the classroom. He refers to Plant (1987, p. 135) who sees maximum involvement by a process of parallel implementation as 'an absolute key to effective management of evolutionary change'.

The sooner the team is in place, the sooner the process of team-building and 'vision building' (Everard and Morris, 1996) can begin. They describe a process whereby staff can build on their own 'scenarios' of what there can be in the future as a way of securing greater commitment and understanding. The process can then be extended to all staff who will be affected. What might emerge then is a statement of 'a core mission'. The underlying assumption is that there are core values that all participants share. These need to be identified and refined early on in the process. In relation to pastoral care, key questions would include: what is the role and value of pastoral care and how does it contribute to the broad educational aims of the school?

Establishing teams also serves to help gain allies. Since change is complex and likely to affect a number of areas, it makes good sense to have 'multiple and consistent leverage points' (Nadler, 1993, p. 93) to fuel the change process. Without active teams and allies, the head of pastoral care or head of PSE can be a lonely figure who has been given responsibility for an area (often in addition to other responsibilities) and who has limited scope for action. The following example demonstrates this clearly.

School D   School D is a 14–18 state comprehensive school. The school is described as having a strong academic tradition with staff particularly committed to their subject teaching. The head of PSE has worked at the school for 20 years and has been responsible for PSE for the last five years. She is on the senior management team as head of Key Stage 4 (and as such, line manager for the heads of year). Referring to the role of head of PSE she states 'This was bolted on to my job. Someone else did it and had a nervous breakdown so they threw it at me and said "You'd better do it, hadn't you?"' A group of staff who originally helped with materials have 'escaped' leaving 'one or two who couldn't get off even if they wanted to'. She goes on to say that she is 'not getting enough (support) in from outside'.

In the case of this teacher, there is a crying need to establish a team, possibly headed by a new head of PSE. Interviews with the teacher reveal that she feels despondent about the situation, unable to see the issues clearly, and does not feel in a strong position to negotiate for change.

Carnall (1995, pp. 44–50) sees the process of managing change as essentially that of problem-solving and consequently devotes a lot of attention to obstacles or 'blocks' to problem-solving and change. He takes his ideas from Adams (1987) who divides 'blocks' into different categories:

- *perceptual blocks*: e.g. an inability to see the issues clearly;
- *emotional blocks*: e.g. the risk of failure and the inability to cope with ambiguity;
- *cultural blocks*: e.g. rigidity of tradition, narrowness of approach to problem-solving and a lack of balance between reason and intuition;
- *environmental blocks*: e.g. a non-supportive environment;
- *cognitive blocks*: e.g. an inflexible use of problem-solving strategies.

There are examples of these blocks in the case study schools. It might be worth looking back at the four examples and trying to identify which blocks might be influencing the change process.

Planning

When developing a 'game plan' a useful starting point might well be the school's Institutional Development Plan (IDP). If aspects of pastoral care policy can be framed in the context of whole school planning, they have a greater likelihood of success. Lodge (1995, p. 27) recommends that 'developmental aspects of the policy (be) clearly indicated in the plan and indications of target dates, expected outcomes and responsibilities (be) allocated to named people'.

Many change efforts are undermined by overambitious objectives. Carnall (1995, p. 15) is particularly pragmatic: 'The "ideal" state will not be achieved. Our view is that through a better understanding we can do a little better, no more!'

The analysis of the needs–provision gap will have revealed the area that needs changing but, at this stage, it is important to be specific and identify exactly what is to be changed and how, and suggest ways in which the changes can be supported and measured. The best results come from smaller, more focused efforts. Fullan (1991) refers to a 'start small, think big' approach which can be adapted to a 'Think big (i.e. look at the big picture) and act small (break down the possible outcomes and decide which ones are feasible, measurable and most beneficial)'.

Acting and reflecting

After detailed preparation, it is time to put the plan into action. This phase should be characterized by systematic monitoring, sustained support for individuals and opportunities for participants to reflect on their work and benefit from appropriate staff development opportunities. Action research (cf. Hopkins, 1993; Elliott, 1991) is a logical vehicle for such work.

Ongoing support is of paramount importance. Although referring to change on a different scale, Huberman and Miles' (1984, p. 273) statement still applies: 'Large scale, change-bearing innovations lived or died by the amount and quality of assistance that their users received once the change process was under way.' Strategies such as mentoring, coaching and action research should be in place and, according to Stoll and Fink (1996, p. 54), 'continuation requires ongoing coordination, problem solving, negotiation, support, communication and sharing of new knowledge'.

Staff should receive regular feedback and there should be regular progress reviews. Monitoring and evaluation are often the weakest areas of activity in schools yet they are important for a variety of reasons:

- they oblige managers and teachers to set targets in the first place;
- they offer yardsticks for the school to know when it has got to where it was supposed to be;
- they signal the end of the change, a point at which different mechanisms come into play to maintain the change;
- they offer a 'ratchet to stop backsliding' (Everard and Morris, 1996, p. 261);
- they help to check on unforeseen consequences of change;
- they allow for reward and recognition for those who have been involved.

CONCLUSION

As we have seen in this chapter, managing change is often extremely messy, complex and fraught with problems and pitfalls. In order to bring about change, schools need to spend much more time and energy on planning in depth rather than tending to rush into the action stage (Beckhard and Harris, 1987). Schools must use their resources wisely and seek the help of outside agents, where possible, who can facilitate, *not* lead, the process. We have seen the need for a carefully negotiated 'game plan' which, while offering a structure within which to operate, nevertheless offers the flexibility to respond to the range of situations and interactions that might arise. The plan might well have 'twists and turns' (Louis and Miles, 1990) but these are to be expected.

Change, generally, is hard to achieve in schools and we have seen that pastoral care presents a unique set of challenges to the management of the school. The complexity of provision, the involvement of all staff, the holistic approach to caring for the whole school community, the difficulties of monitoring and evaluating all combine to make the task a difficult but ultimately most rewarding one.

We must all know headteachers who are committed to pastoral care and who keep 'chipping away' in the hope that they can create the type of school that they want. The message of this chapter is that only by adopting a strategic approach can one realistically bring about meaningful, sustainable change, and only then if the organization has the supportive culture and the capacity to learn.

REFERENCES

Adams, J. L. (1987) *Conceptual Blockbusting*. Harmondsworth: Penguin.

Beckhard, R. and Harris, R. T. (1987) *Organizational Transitions: Managing Complex Change* (2nd edition). Woking: Addison-Wesley.

Bell, L. and Maher, P. (1986) *Leading a Pastoral Team*. Oxford: Blackwell.

Best, R., Lang, P., Lodge, C. and Watkins, C. (eds) (1995) *Pastoral Care and Personal-Social Education: Entitlement and Provision*. London: Cassell.

Calvert, M. and Henderson, J. (1995) Leading the team: managing pastoral care in the secondary setting. In Bell, J. and Harrison, B. (eds) *Vision and Values in Managing Education: Successful Leadership Principles and Practice*, pp. 70–80. London: Fulton.

Carnall, C. A. (1995) *Managing Change in Organizations*. Englewood Cliffs, NJ: Prentice-Hall.

Elliott, J. (1991) *Action Research for Educational Change*. Milton Keynes: Open University Press.

Everard, K. B. and Morris, G. (1996) *Effective School Management*. London: Paul Chapman Publishing.

Fullan, M. (1988) Research into educational innovation. In Glatter, R., Preedy, M. and Riches, C. (eds) *Understanding School Management*. Milton Keynes: Open University Press.

Fullan, M. (1991) *The New Meaning of Educational Change*. New York: Teachers College Press; Toronto: OISE Press and London: Cassell.

Fullan, M. and Hargreaves, A. (1992) *What's Worth Fighting For in Your School?* Milton Keynes: Open University Press/Ontario Public School Teachers' Federation.

Handy, C. (1985) *Understanding Organisations*. London: Penguin.

Hargreaves, A. (1994) *Changing Teachers, Changing Times: Teachers' Work and Culture in the Postmodern Age*. London: Cassell.

Hargreaves, A. and Goodson, I. (1995) Let us take the lead. *Times Educational Supplement*, 24 February.

Hargreaves, D. H. and Hopkins, D. (1991) *The Empowered School*. London: Cassell.

Hopkins, D. (1993) *A Teacher's Guide to Classroom Research* (2nd edition). Buckingham: Open University Press.

Huberman, M. and Miles, M. (1984) *Innovation Up Close*. New York: Plenum.

Ketteringham, J. (1987) Pupils' perceptions of the role of the form tutor. *Pastoral Care in Education*, **5**(3), 206–17.

Lodge, C. (1995) School management for pastoral care and PSE. In Best, R., Lang, P., Lodge, C. and Watkins, C. (eds) *Pastoral Care and Personal-Social Education: Entitlement and Provision*. London: Cassell.

Louis, K. and Miles, M. B. (1990) *Improving the Urban High School: What Works and Why?* New York: Teachers College Press.

McCalman, J. and Paton, R. A. (1992) *Change Management: A Guide to Effective Implementation*. London: Paul Chapman Publishing.

McLaughlin, M. W. (1991) Enabling staff development: what have we learned? In Lieberman, A. and Miller, L. (eds) *Staff Development for Education in the '90s: New Demands, New Realities, New Perspectives*. New York: Teachers College Press, Columbia University.

Marsh, C. (1994) An analysis of selected school improvement practices. In Bennett, N. *et al. Improving Educational Research through Research and Consultancy*. London: Paul Chapman Publishing in Association with the Open University.

Mayon-White, B. (1993) Problem solving in small groups: team members as agents. In Mabey, C. and Mayon-White, B. (eds) *Managing Change*. London: Paul Chapman Publishing in Association with the Open University.

Nadler, D. A. (1993) Concepts for the management of organizational change. In Mabey, C. and Mayon-White, B. (eds) *Managing Change*. London: Paul Chapman Publishing in Association with the Open University.

Oldroyd, D. and Hall, V. (1991) *Managing Staff Development*. London: Paul Chapman.

O'Sullivan, F. (1995) Training and support for pastoral care. In Best, R. *et al.* (eds) *Pastoral Care and Personal-Social Education: Entitlement and Provision*. London: Cassell.

Peters, T. and Waterman, R. (1982) *In Search of Excellence: Lessons from America's Best Run Companies*. London: Harper and Row.

Plant, R. (1987) *Managing Change and Making It Stick*. London: HarperCollins.

Rylance, J. and Evans, G. (1993a) C'mon Everybody Project, Fifth Interim Report to the Home Office. Unpublished.

Rylance, J. and Evans, G. (1993b) C'mon Everybody Project, Second Evaluation Report to the Home Office. Unpublished.

Shaw, M. (1994) Current issues in pastoral management. *Pastoral Care in Education*, **12**(4), 37–41.

Stoll, L. and Fink, D. (1996) *Changing Our Schools*. Buckingham: Open University Press.

TACADE (1994) *Skills for Life: Core Manual*. Manchester: TACADE.

Warner Burke, W. (1987) *Organization Development: A Normative View*. Reading, MA: Addison-Wesley.

CHAPTER 9

The development of understanding in pastoral care: an innovative approach using Interpersonal Process Recall

Jon Scaife

INTRODUCTION

If the 'competence' lobby is to be believed, the National Curriculum in England and Wales can be taught adequately as long as teachers possess appropriate technical skills. The same could hardly be said for the pastoral role in teaching. As Calvert observed in the previous chapter in this book, there is no consensus on curriculum content in pastoral care. Indeed, there is no clear sense that pastoral care *should* be conceptualized in terms of curriculum and still less is there agreement on a set of instrumental competences that are necessary and sufficient for carrying out the pastoral role.

The lower the profile of curriculum content the greater the demands on the practitioner. Stripped of the props that the curriculum provides, the pastoral teacher's great challenge is to be able to work effectively in the essentially interpersonal context of pastoral care. The management of pastoral care, whether in managing or supporting colleagues, or in the pastoral role with students, starts with an understanding of the dynamics of interpersonal processes. This assertion underpins the current chapter. Without such an understanding, what hope can there be that pastoral care is informed, purposeful and effective?

Why is pastoral care said to have low status in teaching? The following explanations have been offered:

1. Teachers are neither trained for, nor competent in, the pastoral role.
2. There is no consensus on what pastoral teaching involves and therefore it cannot be taught; in consequence, it is impossible to assess the effectiveness of pastoral care in schools.
3. Pastoral care is not seen as important by teachers or students.

In this chapter I hope to refute these claims.

In response to the first, it is argued that teachers may be helped to gain understanding and confidence in the interpersonal domain in various ways during the course of initial teacher education and continuing professional development. One of these ways is Interpersonal Process Recall, or IPR, which is discussed and illustrated in detail below. Addressing the second claim, it has already been noted that a national curriculum in pastoral care is not a desirable goal. A lack of curriculum does not prevent pastoral teaching from having intention, direction and purpose. Pastoral teachers may, however, feel uneasy about whether they are doing their jobs properly. How *do* we decide if we are doing our jobs properly? We synthesize our understanding of what we are doing with what we apprehend from the social environment. When the intra- and interpersonal domains approach congruence we know we are doing it properly. The prerequisite for this is understanding – in the case of pastoral care, understanding not of attainment targets nor of competence specifications but of interpersonal processes and societal values. This chapter addresses the issue of improving understanding of interpersonal processes.

Regarding the third claim, for several years, during an initial teacher education programme, I have run a workshop in which student teachers are invited to reflect on things they have learned that are really important to them. They are then asked to talk in small groups about how they came to learn these things. The next stage is for the groups to specify the things they feel it is important that children should learn by the time they leave school. Year on year the resulting wall-charts proclaim the centrality in student teachers' thinking of the personal and social dimensions in children's learning. The only suggestion of curriculum content appears in reference to communication skills. How can it be, then, that pastoral care is not regarded as important in schools? What happens to new teachers' commitment to pastoral care and PSE when they are in post? Have curriculum and assessment become wholly dominant? These are certainly strong concerns that shape teachers' professional lives.

Would-be managers of change in pastoral care will make little headway if they adopt the standpoint that pastoral care is as respectable and important as curriculum teaching. The point has to be insisted upon that pastoral care is *not* curriculum. Teaching it, conceptualizing it – are different. Managing change in pastoral care is *necessarily* different from managing curricular or other school-located change. In particular, pastoral care involves a different kind of understanding from much curriculum teaching, and without radical and reflexive approaches to the management of change, the result will inevitably be cosmetic and temporary. Real change in pastoral care will follow changes in the conceptualization of pastoral care by teachers and managers in schools.

There are many ways of promoting change in teachers' practice. Some of these focus on changing teachers' behaviour *per se*. In only a few approaches is teachers' deeper understanding of their practice regarded as a key to sustained and purposeful change. The method of enquiry known as IPR, employed by teachers to investigate their work, is in this second category. In the following sections I will describe IPR and illustrate its use in three examples. The first, from a continuing professional development programme, is located in a curriculum context (Year 9 geography). The issue for the teacher, however, was unrelated to the subject. In using IPR for the first time, the teacher was investigating interactions in his class. In so doing he was improving his understanding of student–teacher relationships. This is central to the pastoral role. The second example examines a teacher's use of IPR to evaluate the effectiveness of her tutorial programme in a novel way. The third example describes the experiences of student teachers who used IPR to develop their understanding of interpersonal processes in school contexts.

In comparison with other methods, frameworks or approaches that might typically be encountered in the professional development of teachers, IPR is unusual in certain respects. Firstly, it is free of content. IPR was not designed with a particular curriculum in mind, or a particular view of learning or schooling. In fact, although it has been used in contexts as diverse as education, the armed forces, the church, counselling, the emergency services, government and elsewhere, IPR was not designed particularly for any of these. It is flexible and adaptable.

Secondly, IPR depends on people listening to each other and making enquiries in non-judgemental ways rather than on people telling each other things. When in a pastoral role (in interaction with students or with colleagues) teachers operate in a world of knowledge and values that is distinct from the familiar, everyday context of curriculum and administration. A teacher in the 'pastoral world' may be a listener, a non-judgemental explorer and a respecter of the views, values and histories of others. Because these role behaviours are characteristic of the IPR process, IPR lends itself particularly well to application in the development of practice and understanding in pastoral care.

A crucial factor in the effectiveness of IPR in the continuing professional development projects described below was the role of school management in contributing to the construction of a supportive professional context for the teachers' self-enquiry. In looking deeply at their own practice, the teachers knew that they were taking risks and it is unlikely that they would have done this without trust and confidence in their senior colleagues. I will attempt to draw from these cases how this climate of trust came about. I will also suggest how IPR can contribute to the education of newly- and pre-qualified teachers and to more effective pastoral care in schools.

WHAT IS IPR?

Briefly, IPR is a method by which people can learn about interpersonal processes. Its originator, Norman Kagan (Kagan, 1984, 1988), described it as 'a method for improving human understanding'. It works by drawing on people's memories of tape-recorded interactions in which they have taken part. The recall of these interactions is helped by the replay of the recording (video or audio). In addition the recall is supported by someone who was not involved in the recorded interactions. This person is known in IPR as the 'enquirer'. It is the enquirer's role to ask questions of the recaller (or recallers), to facilitate their understanding of the interactions that were recorded on the tape. A distinctive feature of the method is that it is the recaller's ideas about the interaction that are given prominence. The enquirer does not attempt to contribute her or his own ideas about the interaction. Examples might be: What did you hope to communicate then? What thoughts were going through your mind at the time? Did you know how the others felt? Was there anything that you wanted to happen? Did the setting affect you in any way? The purpose for the enquiry may be established by the recaller or may be left unspecified; it is not set by the enquirer, whose questions tend to be 'content-free' and non-judgemental.

The use of IPR is illustrated further in the examples described in this chapter. Fuller details of the method may be found in Kagan and Kagan (1991).

CONTINUING PROFESSIONAL DEVELOPMENT: OPEN ENQUIRY

This section describes how IPR was taken up by teachers as part of a programme of professional development introduced by a new head-teacher. Soon after his appointment, the head of the school established a programme of professional development projects. Each year staff were invited to participate in the forthcoming year's project if they felt that it addressed their needs. Projects were not tightly defined. The following example, in which Steve, a member of the geography department, participated, was called 'The Performing Art of Teaching'. It was the head's intention in that year to move the emphasis towards classroom practice from the preceding themes of curriculum development and policy review. This flexibility probably contributed to the willingness of staff to take part.

The school is a medium-sized 11–18 comprehensive school, three miles outside a city. Steve was a senior teacher. Other participants in the new project included two in their second year of teaching, several staff with more experience and a head of department. The project was to be guided (a more appropriate term in the event than 'led') by myself and a colleague, both tutors from a university education department in the region.

Self-motivated teacher engagement in the project was regarded as crucial by the university staff and the headteacher. Once this was acknowledged, serious doubt was cast over the extent to which the content of a project such as this could be specified in advance. The only needs that could reliably be identified belonged to those doing the identifying (ourselves): anything else would be guesswork. At this point the headteacher might have argued that, through his responsibility for the school as a whole, he should specify how he wished the participating staff to be 'developed'. He declined to do this. On reflection, this decision was essential for the subsequent autonomy of the staff involved in the project.

In the absence of a content-based agenda, the staff development project began with various activities which were intended to elicit participants' perceived needs and aspirations within the broad scope of 'the performing art of teaching'. These activities are reported in detail in Lally and Scaife (1995). What emerged was the clear capability of participants to define their own projects. The key was the management decision that resulted in the teachers having enough professional space to be able to reflect on, and share aspects of, their current practice and its history. Some participants reported their last experience of creative, as opposed to reactive, professional dialogue to have been during their initial teacher education.

In one of the early activities during the whole-group introduction to the project, participants volunteered to be video recorded while teaching the rest of the group on topics of their own choice. These 'mini-lessons', which lasted for approximately ten minutes, were conducted with a view to experimenting with IPR. As I was to take the role of IPR enquirer during replay of the tape I was not present during the recordings. The reason for the enquirer's absence during recording is to help the enquirer to focus on facilitating the recall, rather than becoming involved – even unwittingly – in the content of the recording. My task was to assist the recall process by asking helpful questions of the recallers and by keeping the focus of discussion on events in the past – generally around the time at which the recording was made. This point may appear rather odd. It is based, however, on the simple idea that each individual is capable of unique insight into her or his own past thoughts and feelings. Each one of us has 'expert' awareness of, and access to, our personal self, at least in comparison with the knowledge we have of other people's innermost thoughts and feelings. Because of this, when it comes to recall, we are all more or less on an equal footing: hierarchies that may operate in the everyday world do not apply in the past tense of recall in IPR.

The enquirer explains to those watching the tape (the 'recallers') that they are in charge of the playback of the tape and that whenever a thought or a feeling occurs to someone that they would like to explore, dwell on or describe, they should stop the tape, or ask the enquirer to stop it. (The enquirer only stops the tape when asked by a recaller.) Initially, recallers may be reticent but this rapidly diminishes after the tape has been stopped for the first time. Invariably, recallers are surprised by the depth of exploration made possible in IPR. They remark on how much is 'going on', even in apparently mundane interactions between people. This is one of the pillars on which IPR rests: that in normal human interaction, thoughts and feelings are much quicker than words. Ideas follow each other so rapidly that we can only dwell or reflect on a few, while others escape our close attention. Our understanding of interactions is inevitably piecemeal. When we find a 'gap', we are good at making guesses – but we are fallible. In complex or difficult interactions our guesses may be 'wrong', unhelpful or counterproductive. If only we were able to return to the original interaction and reflect on it more slowly, then perhaps we could come to a better understanding of it. The assumption that this is likely to improve human interactions is a second pillar on which IPR stands.

After the mini-lessons, some of the project teachers were interested in using IPR to explore processes in their teaching. Others found it too daunting or risky. The prospect of finding things out can sometimes feel very threatening. One teacher declared early on that he was 'not ready to be videoed'. (Later in the year, however, having filmed a departmental colleague, he initiated the recording of his own teaching.)

Steve decided to use IPR with a Y9 geography class. He was particularly interested to learn about his interactions with the students. Steve asked a colleague to film him and several days later he and I met for an IPR session.[1] On watching the tape he found much to recall: 'I was staggered by ... the many things on the screen that [made me want] to stop it and recall the whole process of what was going on.' The recall process provided Steve with abundant data about his teaching but he repeatedly found himself wondering what effect his actions had had on the students. He decided that if he really wanted to know, he would need to involve them in the recall process and so he asked the class for volunteers. It is not difficult to obtain student volunteers for IPR recall because they tend to be keen to see video recordings of themselves. But it can be a daunting step for the teacher to take, as Steve found: 'I was slightly nervous about doing that. I thought it was a risk I was taking and to a certain extent the students were taking a risk as well.'

The group recall involved Steve and six students. One of the characteristics of IPR is that each recaller is regarded as an *expert as far as her or his own thoughts and feelings are concerned*. This apparently simple axiom has a remarkable emancipatory effect. Irrespective of the recallers' relationship outside IPR, the dialogue during recall tends to be respectful, insightful and heterarchical. Reflecting later on the group recall, Steve commented:

That was quite illuminating; so much so that a couple of the group ... their perspectives were ones that frankly I would have been proud of if I was an educationalist in there looking at the lesson. They were judgemental but not damningly judgemental.

Steve was used to interacting with this class as a group of normal Y9 children, novices at his curriculum subject, who demanded from him the usual repertoire of managing, controlling, motivating. It is no exaggeration to report, however, that the perception and maturity of these same students during recall astounded him. They were thoughtful, insightful and considered in their accounts of their experiences in the lesson they were reflecting upon. It was as if they had become different people. He remarked that he had experienced 'nothing like it in eleven years of teaching'.

As part of the staff development project, a follow-up interview with Steve took place eleven weeks after the group recall. He reported that a difference had emerged in the way that the students who participated in the recall now interacted with him. One boy who previously used to pass Steve in the school corridors as if he did not exist now made confident eye contact and acknowledged him verbally. He felt that the students had valued the confidence that he had shown in them: 'I think [it] has been hugely beneficial to that group. ... We've got a more cemented relationship because of that.'

Steve's experiment with IPR encouraged other teachers to do the same in the staff development projects that followed. The method is now an option in the school's approach to professional development. Perhaps more significantly, the values underpinning IPR have become a part of the school's culture.

CONTINUING PROFESSIONAL DEVELOPMENT: EVALUATING PASTORAL STUDIES

In the year following Steve's project, Lesley, a science teacher in her second year in post, took up IPR for the specific purpose of evaluating 'active tutorial work'. This was the programme of work undertaken in tutor group periods. Lesley had felt inadequately prepared by her Initial Teacher Education course for teaching pastoral studies and other aspects of the tutor's role. Her experience in the first year of teaching had left her uncertain about the effectiveness of her interpretation of the pastoral programme. The programme was evaluated by the students but Lesley was unwilling to rely on the results. One of the issues was the timing of the evaluation: questionnaires were issued at the end of the academic year and student self-evaluation took place at the same time as school reports were being compiled. Timing was not her only concern, however; she felt that students' awareness of their own learning in pastoral studies (their 'meta-learning') tended to be sketchy. They found difficulty in composing and expressing evaluative comments: 'when dealing with work on a more abstract level it is difficult to state how useful it is'. Instead, students were reporting things that they thought the teacher wanted to hear. Lesley's view was that this could lead to the perpetuation of ineffective approaches to pastoral studies:

I feel there is a need to develop a strategy which will allow the students to comment freely on their experiences during active tutorial work [and] which will allow the tutor to ask questions and gain a full understanding of the individuals and the tutor group as a whole.

Steve had used IPR for self-directed discovery learning. Lesley, by contrast, had specific lines of enquiry from the start. Following topic work in the tutorials, she had identified the following questions:

1 Did the students show an understanding of the topic?

2 Did the work develop any new ideas about the topic?

3 Had their ideas and opinions concerning the topic changed and were such changes the result of work done in the tutorials?

Lesley suspected that some of her 21 Year 8 students might act up for the video camera at first and so she introduced it into tutorials before she needed it for IPR. The session she recorded for use in IPR was a series of student presentations on healthy living, with the students playing various roles. Reflecting on the session soon afterwards she reported a sense of disappointment. She felt that the combination of student role-playing, student presentations and filming was too much for some members of the group. IPR is surprisingly robust, however, as far as the content and quality of recording are concerned. Even quite poor stimuli can trigger detailed recall. Lesley found that, despite her pessimism about the tape prior to recall, it turned out to be surprisingly inform-ative:

There was a lot of useful data to glean from the footage. I was able to recall the events well and even to reflect on actual feelings throughout the session . . . there were many areas which needed explanation from the students involved, concerning areas covered during the topic and actions of individuals on the tape.

After Lesley's individual recall she decided to ask for volunteers from the tutor group to join her for a group recall. As in Steve's class there were more than enough volunteers. Lesley decided to pick six students from different friendship groups. The group recall turned out to be fruitful:

The comments which the students made were surprisingly mature ... after initial apprehension all six spoke freely .... The main comments were very positive and allowed an insight into the interactions with the tutor group as a whole.

Lesley summarized the students' views from the recall session as follows:

1. Students did find tutorial work 'useful'; however, they did find that at times areas were covered which they already understood.
2. The students felt that the active tutorial sessions allowed them to discuss their own views and to try to understand other points of view which they then adopted if they agreed with them.
3. The students informed me that I allowed certain members of the group to dominate discussion work at times. However, I did allow all who had something to say to do so.
4. The students expressed the view that they enjoyed not spending too long on any one topic. They also enjoyed moving to topics which were clearly different from the last.
5. Students felt group work to be more beneficial and enjoyable than individual or written work, i.e. worksheets.

This set of summary points represents the achievement of Lesley's goal in the staff development project. She had set out to investigate whether IPR could provide her with more reliable feedback from her students on which she could take action. She felt she had accomplished this task.

SUCCESSFUL USE OF IPR IN SCHOOL

Lesley and Steve felt that their experiments with IPR had been successful. Several factors appear to have contributed to this:

- The teachers were – and were encouraged to be – inquisitive about aspects of teaching and learning.
- The staff development project allowed teachers time to reflect on their practice and to clarify particular issues for further enquiry.
- The fact that there was a project group, as opposed to individuals working alone, helped to sustain momentum.
- The headteacher's decision to define only the broad theme of the project gave scope for teachers to focus on their own perceived needs and interests.
- The agenda for the early meetings of the project group was focused on enquiring, rather than on completing tasks. (It is worth noting that this approach did, though, lead to the completion of project tasks!)

- Participants were expected to provide feedback on the project work to the rest of the staff, including the senior management team.
- Participation in the project was voluntary.
- Funding was provided for supply cover to release participants from some of their teaching on the ten project days (on average, one or two double periods from an eight-period day).
- The headteacher's approach to the project mirrored the project itself. His agenda was enquiry-based, not directive. Leadership was subtly expressed through the expectation that staff would take control and direct their own projects. His hands-off orientation was welcomed by staff, except towards the end of the projects. At this stage, senior management team involvement was sought in order that ideas generated during the projects might come to influence decisions on future policy. Participants' commitment to their development work was clearly evident here.
- The social-professional culture in the school was tolerant towards staff development. Colleagues were willing to swap rooms, lend equipment and generally help out in support.

In the IPR-based projects, teachers were willing to take risks in order to learn from their students. A crucial contributory factor here seems to be the perception of a positive social-professional culture in which teachers are confident of support from peers and managers. Additionally, the teachers who used IPR were curious about the thoughts and feelings of their students and they accorded them value. It is probably not coincidental that the message from the school management to the project participants was similar: the teachers' needs and aspirations were acknowledged, accommodated and valued.

INTRODUCING IPR TO NEW TEACHERS

The results obtained from IPR by practising teachers suggest that this is a practicable and effective method of enquiry. But how crucial is it for teachers to have had professional experience before using it? Could IPR have anything to offer in the personal and professional development of pre-qualified teachers? Reforms in the structure of initial teacher education (ITE) courses (DfE, 1992; CATE, 1992) have shifted the emphasis in student teaching strongly towards school-based practical experience, with a corresponding reduction in the proportion of time spent studying education. In the university-based part of their PGCE course (currently twelve weeks), students are expected to learn as much as they can in preparation for their periods of school experience. Inevitably, much of this time is dominated by concerns about acquiring skills and strategies for managing classes, preparing lessons and teaching the National Curriculum. It is no wonder that the 'ologies' have been all but squeezed out! Many teacher educators, however, remain committed to the idea that ITE involves more than simply inducting graduates into the role of curriculum 'deliverers'. Interest in issues such as personal and social development, pupil–teacher relationships and how people learn remains high, despite systematic attempts to marginalize them in the education 'market'.

EDUCATIONAL AND PROFESSIONAL STUDIES

This section describes how an IPR workshop was included in an Education Fair for student teachers nearing the end of their PGCE course. The Fair itself was an attempt to integrate some 'marginal' issues within the PGCE course. The aims and the format of the workshop are described and evaluative comments of the participants are reported.

The taught component of the Sheffield PGCE course consists of two main strands. One is subject-related and the other, EPS, concerns issues that are not strongly subject-specific. A rough parallel could have been drawn between these strands and the responses of two imaginary teachers who, when asked to describe their jobs, said 'I teach Chemistry' and 'I teach children'. The EPS course stresses pupil–teacher relationships, equity, special needs and the teacher's pastoral role, as well as the student teacher's individual interests and concerns and the tutor's specialisms. Diversity and choice can be more readily built in when the curriculum is not dominated by subject matter. The EPS course reflects this. Students and tutors are jointly responsible for constructing the week-by-week seminar activities. In particular, towards the end of the course, students' experiences of studying education and practising teaching often result in the emergence of interests that fall outside mainstream curriculum concerns. In an attempt to respond to and to stimulate students' more esoteric interests the tutor team incorporated an Education Fair into the EPS course. Students were asked to opt into workshops from a choice that included, among other themes, stress and time management, Alexander technique, alternative educational provision for pupils with learning difficulties, VSO, development education, issues of sexuality, and IPR.

An introductory workshop on IPR

My own introduction to IPR was through processes of activity and exploration in a workshop led by its originator, Norman Kagan. This encouraged me to adopt a similar approach. The aim in the PGCE workshop, therefore, was to situate both the practice and the theory of IPR within a context that was familiar and relevant to the participants, namely, teaching.

Student teachers seem generally quite well disposed towards peer teaching and to the use of video. As a result, a colleague and I decided that we would ask for volunteers to teach brief 'lessons' to groups of around six others. The choice of topic was left to the volunteers. There were roughly 14 participants for each of the half-day workshops and so we had two 'lessons' in the morning and two in the afternoon. In each case the students operated the video camera, set the lesson context and conducted the lesson, the only constraint being that they had 15 minutes in which to complete it. It was not difficult to obtain volunteer teachers. This may have been due in part to the free choice of teaching topic, which is something of a novelty in these curriculum-driven times! The topics chosen on this occasion were the LBW rule in cricket, the physiology of speech, earth science and the pottery industry, and martial arts.

The experience of participating in lesson simulations is repeatedly reported as being enjoyable and interesting, not only for those in the teacher role but also for the class. In the IPR workshops the simulations were successful in providing an active and up-beat beginning. They also set the scene: participants were curious about what was going to happen next.

Peter, my colleague, had been absent during the filming as he was to take the role of 'enquirer' in the subsequent recall. In his introduction to the recall process, Peter included some encouraging words about stopping the video tape and in both workshops within three or four minutes someone had intervened. Once the ice is broken in recall, participants tend to become energized, as was the case in these workshops. We found that, although our intention had been only to introduce IPR as a method of enquiry, the student teachers became engaged in the content of the recall. One of the lesson simulations, despite occupying only ten minutes of tape, generated highly illuminating and thoughtful discussion about gender and the teacher–student interactions that had taken place.

Student teachers' reactions to IPR

Participants were invited to complete evaluation questionnaires anonymously. In all, 24 were returned from a possible 28. They were asked to rate their *interest in* and *enjoyment of* the workshop. There were no negative responses, two qualified responses and 22 unqualified positive responses. Asked to rate the perceived relevance of IPR to their professional development, participants gave no negative responses (i.e. nobody rated it as irrelevant), 13 gave qualified replies such as 'fairly relevant' and eleven gave unqualified positive responses. They were also invited to make general evaluative comments, a cross-section of which is included below:

- Relevant, in that I am interested in my behaviour with other people and their impression of me – surely invaluable for teaching.
- Very good way of assessing development and improving awareness in the classroom.
- Would like to try it at school, worried about lack of time.
- I am very interested in the way relationships between teachers and pupils are formed and by learning from today, this would enhance my relationship with pupils ... I would have liked to take part in it early on in the year so that I could have expert help in the classroom situation.
- Relevant in an abstract way, but I feel I would like to use the technique when I begin teaching.
- I will go on thinking about it and it will be of use in the future. I think this would be of value to everyone.
- It has made me more aware of possible relationships within my classroom. It made me think. We were all involved.

Reflections on introducing IPR in the workshop
In running the workshop we hoped to shed light on several questions:

1. Could we fit a reasonable introduction to IPR into a half-day session?
2. Could we find a way of introducing IPR that was informative, engaging and consistent with IPR itself?
3. Would new teachers regard IPR as marginal to their currently perceived needs?

The first issue remains unclear. Several participants commented in their evaluations that a whole day would have been more appropriate and one person mentioned leaving with a sense of unanswered questions. Is this necessarily a 'bad thing'? Is it more appropriate for the workshop to suggest that the reserves of human experience which IPR explores are vastly subtle and complex, and there will probably always be unanswered questions? There is another sense in which it may be desirable to avoid the implication that IPR can be 'done in a day' (like 'doing Europe in a week'!). When particular days in a course are labelled 'Equal Opportunities' or 'Special Educational Needs' the impression can sometimes be formed that 'that's it – I've done Equal Opps. now'. The corollary is that equal opportunities/special needs are no longer issues and, therefore, can be forgotten about. If, by 'doing' IPR in a day, participants feel human interactions had been covered, then the introduction would have been counterproductive.

The second of the above questions can be answered positively. The evaluative comments showed a high level of interest. Their engagement with recall, and their subsequent reflection on this process, suggested that participants had gained some operational understanding of IPR. The question of consistency between the medium and the message puts workshop leaders on their mettle. It would be inconsistent, for instance, for the leaders to do a lot of 'telling'. A more appropriate approach would perhaps be to enquire: to ask questions of the participants and to support them in their questioning of the workshop leaders.

On the basis of the student teachers' evaluative comments, the third question can be answered confidently: No! They made it clear that the interpersonal dimension in teaching is a matter of interest and concern to them.

IPR IN THE PROFESSIONAL DEVELOPMENT OF TEACHERS: SOME REFLECTIONS

There are several ways in which IPR might be used in an educational setting. The approach taken by Steve was to use it for *open-ended enquiry*. He had no fixed questions at the outset and decided to treat IPR as something new to be explored. The outcome of individual recall was that Steve accumulated information and impressions that gave him a new perspective on his teaching. Individual recall also helped him to define lines of enquiry into his classroom practice which he subsequently chose to follow up through group recall with some of his students. Steve's experiment with IPR resulted in him changing his views of his students' capacity for insight and mature reflection. It also led to general improvement in his relationships with students in the participating class.

In contrast with Steve, Lesley took a goal-directed approach in her use of IPR. Through her tutor group teaching she had already defined various lines of enquiry that she wanted to follow in order to evaluate the tutorial programme. Individual recall gave her enough confidence in IPR for her to take part in group recall with the students. She regarded the outcome as a more honest and more useful evaluation of the students' learning in PSE.

Another instance of IPR used in evaluation was reported by Marsh (1983). The course was a series of training sessions for trainers, not unlike some versions of in-service teacher training. It became increasingly clear to the course leader that the participants' learning was being strongly influenced by their dominant affective state – boredom! Marsh hypothesized that there was a dissonance between the leader's adoption of an open-learning approach and the participants' desire for a directed, didactic style of training. She used IPR to investigate this and to examine the effects of boredom as a barrier to learning.

The IPR workshop for student teachers was designed to raise the issue of self-directed enquiry into the effects and the effectiveness of teaching. The student teachers approached it principally out of curiosity: 'What's this IPR thing ... is there anything in it for me?' The views emerged clearly that they felt that it *is* important to enquire into the effects of teaching and that IPR offers a way of doing so. The first point is not trivial. Many students begin their initial teacher education courses utterly preoccupied with 'survival' in the classroom. They progress by learning to see much more in teaching than just survival but even by the end of the course the focus of attention is often on the teaching performance *per se*. For new teachers, an introduction to IPR may help to bridge the gap between teaching and its impact on children.

IPR was introduced to practising teachers by Burke and Kagan (1976) as a skill in its own right. They found that teachers who became familiar with IPR began to re-evaluate their roles as teachers and as colleagues of teachers:

Over a decade ago, John Holt reported in a popular book, *How Children Fail*, that it was his observation that as teachers 'we are not honest about ourselves, our own fears, limitations, weaknesses, prejudices, motives. We present ourselves to children as if we were gods, all-knowing, all powerful, always rational, always just, always right.' Throughout the project, it was precisely this perception of themselves that teachers reported that they were discarding after IPR training. Over and over again, teachers who had completed the training told us how much better their relationships with their classes were: and, when we asked them to tell us in what ways these relationships had improved, they reported the relief they felt at giving up always being the only expert in the class. They reported how refreshing it was to admit to their students that they didn't know something or that they had made a mistake. What seemed to be happening was that these teachers had examined their 'nightmares' of failing before their students and colleagues in IPR recall sessions; and, as a result, had found that their fears of failure were not the monsters they had believed them to be .... Teachers after the

IPR training seemed less concerned with protecting themselves and more able to focus on the communication process between themselves and their students. This openness also applied to the relationship between teachers. One principal observed that 'teacher-to-teacher relations seem to be more caring'.

A view is held in some quarters that teaching is about 'delivering' a curriculum. It has also been suggested that the effectiveness of teaching can be measured by rating teaching performance against an atomistic set of competence descriptors. These views trivialize the infinitely complex relationship between teaching and learning (in a full sense of the word). No sensible account of what teaching is about can neglect consideration of its intended and its actual effects. Reflection and analysis, using methods such as IPR, acknowledge the subtlety and complexity of teaching that are liable to be overlooked in these careless and mechanistic times.

NOTE

1 The time lag between filming and recall is not crucial in IPR. Norman Kagan, the originator of the method, described a case in which IPR recall by fire-fighters took place a year after filming.

REFERENCES

Burke, J. B. and Kagan, N. I. (1976) *Influencing Human Interaction in Public School*. Project number MH 13526–02. Final Report. Michigan State University College of Education.

Council for the Accreditation of Teacher Education (1992) *The Accreditation of Initial Teacher Training under Circulars 9/92 (DfE) and 35/92 (Welsh Office)*. November. London: Department for Education.

Department for Education (DfE) (1992) *Circular 9/92: Initial Teacher Training (Secondary Phase)*. 25 June. London: Department for Education.

Douglas, B. (1991) Teachers as experts: a case study of school-based staff development. In Bell, L. and Day, C. (eds) *Managing the Professional Development of Teachers, Developing Teachers and Teaching*, pp. 88–109. Milton Keynes: Open University Press.

Kagan, N. (1984) Interpersonal Process Recall: basic methods and recent research. In Larsen, D. (ed.) *Teaching Psychological Skills*, ch. 11, pp. 229–44. Monterey, CA: Brooks Cole.

Kagan, N. (1988) Teaching counselling skills. In Cox, K. R. and Ewan, C. E. (eds) *The Medical Teacher*. Edinburgh: Churchill Livingston.

Kagan, N. I. and Kagan, H. (1991) IPR – a research/training model. In Dowrick, P. N. and associates, *A Practical Guide to Using Video in the Behavioural Sciences*. Canada: Wiley.

Lally, V. and Scaife, J. A. (1995) Towards a collaborative approach to teacher empowerment. *British Educational Research Journal*, **21**(3), 323–38.

Marsh, J. (1983) The boredom of study: a study of boredom. *Management Education and Development*, **14**(2), 120–35.

Conclusion

Mike Calvert and Jenny Henderson

Pastoral care has undergone dramatic changes in the last thirty years and continues to evolve. Developments in thought and practice provide us with important signposts towards a possible future. The different contributors to this book are either modelling good practice in their own schools or, by dint of their research activity, can tap into good practice. Megahy, a recently appointed head in a challenging school, has approached a daunting task with vision and energy. Committed to a belief that pastoral care should support learning, he set out to combat low standards and low expectations by changing roles and responsibilities. He adopts a holistic approach to school development planning and refuses to accept an academic/pastoral divide. Downes, a recently retired head of a very different school, illustrates how he arrived at, and justified, an 'expensive' model of pastoral care and shows how changes in staffing structure, etc. can bring about improved provision.

The heads and staff of the case study schools in Chapter 5 have had to come to terms with a deteriorating social and economic fabric at a time of changes in legislation and upheaval in some of the support agencies. Maximizing the available resources has been seen to be essential in their cases. Wilcox and Taylor show how schools can make the most of inspections and develop the framework to encompass ongoing self-evaluation. Hall and Skelton appeal for caring and equal opportunities, respectively, to underpin practices in school and Calvert offers a mechanism for change which is manageable and sustainable, provided there is the commitment to change and the climate in which to bring it about. Scaife shows how reflection must be an integral part of staff development since so much of pastoral care is based on values and attitudes and these cannot be listed (like competencies) or learnt (like facts).

Bell and Maher's (1986) reference to four stages, the priorities of which are succinctly summed up by Harrison (p. 16) as respectively to: provide a *control mechanism*; to meet *individual needs* of pupils; to develop *group activity* and to devise a *pastoral curriculum* prompts us to ask what the next stage or generation might look like. Looking ahead to the future, it is tempting to quote the surely apocryphal story of the man who, when asking the way to Donegal, was told 'If I were going to Donegal, I wouldn't start from here'. Pastoral care has developed incrementally in a variety of ways, reflecting different traditions and attitudes and different priorities. Not only is pastoral care different in all schools but it is worth bearing in mind that 'the pastoral structure within which most pastoral care managers work will contain elements of all four generations of pastoral care and that various members of the pastoral team may, at least initially, subscribe to different elements of those generations' (Bell and Maher, 1986, p. 12). Although this was written over ten years ago, evidence such as that of Megahy would suggest that the same could be said today of the situation in a large number of schools.

Recent years have seen a move to market forces with its emphasis on academic achievement and accountability and a narrowly-defined curriculum that has threatened to stifle imaginative, holistic approaches to curriculum design. While this shift has affected all schools and areas of school life, there has been a growing realization among many teachers and managers that the market-driven approach can be limited and detrimental to pupils' education. It is possible to detect a growing realization that schools need to look again at their pastoral provision and see how they can improve the personal and social development and, with it, the academic achievement of their pupils.

While the pattern of provision in pastoral care is arguably still as varied and uneven as it ever has been, there are a number of trends in thought which unite many of those who write about the subjects of management and pastoral care and which might offer a way forward in terms of general principles.

ESSENTIAL CHARACTERISTICS

For a school to have a strong pastoral provision the following characteristics would seem indispensable:

- a head and senior management with a vision;
- values that are clearly understood, articulated and shared by the teachers and pupils;
- workable, flexible structures;
- a culture supportive of change and diversity;
- a strategic approach to managing change;
- a willingness to reflect critically on our aims, objectives and effectiveness;
- a clear notion of what care is and of its relation to learning.

To begin with, it should be taken as a given that all heads have a *vision* of what they want their institution to be. 'No good school has been created without ... a vision, and no school continues to be good once the vision of those who lead it has been lost' (Trethowan, 1991, p. 3, quoted in Bell and Harrison, 1995, p. 2). Yet to have a vision is not in itself enough. It has to 'be talked down to earth' (Trethowan, ibid., p. 1) The vision must contain *values* that can be articulated clearly and agreed upon by others. In order to make those values work there is a need for *workable structures*. Teams should replace hierarchies wherever possible, and flexibility and good communication, backed by regular review and evaluation, should be the norm. None of this will be possible without a *culture* based on a climate of trust, empowerment and confidence to support it. For the necessary changes to come about, *strategic planning*, sensitive to the needs and context of the school, is essential if we are to avoid the incrementalism that has characterized developments over the last thirty years. Strategic planning will not come about without an *ability to reflect* on our values and practices. All this will be informed by clear notions of what *caring* means in an educational context.

As one head said when asked about the future of pastoral care, 'there is everything to play for'. Given the lack of support at a national level it is up to each school to determine how it should move forward. The task is not an easy one. Whatever model of provision emerges in the future, it will certainly need to be more complex and sophisticated than previous models and make new demands on teachers and managers. The alternative is to keep 'chugging along'. Surely not.

REFERENCES

Bell, J. and Harrison, B. T. (1995) *Vision and Values in Managing Education: Successful Leadership Principles and Practice*. London: David Fulton Publishers.

Bell, L. and Maher, P. (1986) *Leading a Pastoral Team*. Oxford: Blackwell.

Trethowan, D. M. (1991) *Achieving Quality Schools Through Performance Management*. London: Paul Chapman Publishing.

Name index

Subject index